Fully Human, Fully Divine

AN **ADVENT DEVOTIONAL** FOR THE **WHOLE SELF**

Whitney R. Simpson

UPPER
ROOM BOOKS®
NASHVILLE

To my dad, Ken Rushlow, who embodied and spread hope, peace, love, and joy for all his earthly days.

AN ADVENT POEM

We wait.
We notice.
We sense.
We remember.
We anticipate.
With our whole selves, we seek hope, peace, joy, and love.
They are within our reach, yet we often rush past
    and miss them.
Will we choose to slow down and embody these gifts,
    like the wise ones?
Yes, indeed! We are wise ones.
Help us get ready; open us up, Lord.
Give us the willingness to pause and prepare to receive
    your gift this season.
Let us embody what we discover as we await the divine.
Let us savor your hope, peace, joy, and love
    more fully this season.

CONTENTS

Week 3: Sit with Joy 81

Week 4: Savor God's Love 97

INTRODUCTION

"Christmas is waiting to be born: in
you, in me, in all mankind."
—Howard Thurman[1]

You can feel it. When Christmas is approaching, it is literally in the air. The chill you feel, that snap of the winter wind. It is bracing. It makes you realize the warmth of your own body and appreciate your favorite sweater. It reminds you to feel alert, awake, and alive.

You can see it. The darkness grows longer and longer as the dawn takes its time to arrive each morning and the sun rushes to hurry out of the sky at night. But that same darkness also invites a special kind of seasonal joy, creating a backdrop for the twinkling lights and charming decorations of our homes and the homes of our neighbors. It reminds you to take a look around.

You can smell it and even taste it too. The sweet scent of peppermint filling the air, the alluring aroma of cookies baking; the smells fill your lungs. They bring back memories and create new ones all at once. The taste of a family recipe passed on from generation to generation, the crunch of a candy cane during the one time of year when it is acceptable to eat candy like you're a kid again, the flavors flood your watering mouth. It reminds you to savor it all.

Finally, you can hear it. Not just in the omnipresent Christmas music and the hymns at church, but in the stillness of the earth.

If you take a step outside in the middle of that dark night and simply pause, you'll hear it in the silence, the anticipation, the waiting, the feeling like the entire earth is taking a deep breath, slowly inhaling and exhaling, standing on the edge of whatever comes next. It reminds you to listen.

Advent is the time when Christmas is approaching, and it is a season of memories and anticipation. It is a time that is all about waiting and preparation. Advent encompasses the four weeks leading up to Christmas and is the first season of our Christian year. The word itself comes from the Latin word *adventus*, which means "arrival." Advent is an opportunity to prepare for God to come into our midst, to prepare for God to become human just like us. It is a time when we get ready to celebrate the birth of Christ; a time to invite hope, peace, joy, and love more fully into our lives. What we are waiting for has not yet arrived, but it is coming and it is divine. Do you feel it?

In this devotional, you are invited to experience an embodied Advent that seeks to connect you with your whole self, both your humanity and the spark of divinity that God has given you. Through the four themes of hope, peace, joy, and love, you are invited to wait and encounter God with your whole self. Each week will focus on a theme, and you will be provided with daily contemplative practices and mindfulness techniques to engage your entire body. The prompts and prayers in this book are created with purpose, designed to help you engage and embody this season with your whole self. Each of the daily practices is created to be accessible for both beginners and the most practiced contemplatives in order to connect with both God and your own body this

Advent season. Whether Advent is familiar to you or brand new, this experience invites you to be present with God as you savor this time before Christmas.

Ponder for a moment. How have you prepared for Christmas during the season of Advent in the past? Recall how your traditions have changed, or not, through the years. Consider what you desire this Advent to look like. Are you ready to embrace this time of waiting with your whole self? Since you are reading this book, you have already taken the first step toward an embodied experience this season, and I cannot wait to journey with you!

The expectations that come along with this season can be frustrating or overwhelming, but the great parts of this season are abundant! Personally, I delight in Advent calendars, cozy pajamas, warm fires, hot tea, twinkling white lights, unique ornaments, praying over photo cards, and collecting nativity scenes. I savor the humming of carols, the smell of cinnamon, the bubbling of homemade cranberry sauce, and singing along with favorite Christmas hymns and carols on the kitchen speaker while cooking or baking. I actually enjoy wrapping gifts (I know, not everyone's favorite activity, but I find it meditative rather than frustrating) and always anticipate Christmas Eve service. I love this season! I love how Advent reminds us of what is important and prepares us for what is to come. That's why I am inviting you to join me on this Advent journey to embody the gift of Christ with your whole self.

Before you continue reading, pause for a moment. Take a deep breath in, then exhale slowly. With that breath, you just connected with the divine spark that is within you! It's easy to lose touch and get swept up by the season and forget the breath of life that God has placed inside each of us. So many of us have lost touch with our bodies, with who we were created to be. But no more! Today, you can embrace the challenge and the opportunity of being fully present for Advent as we prepare with anticipation for the birth of Christ, of God being made human.

We are all tempted to cling to the commercialism of Christmas, to fill this season with expectations and tasks. It is easy to do. Often, the whirlwind of these expectations causes us to rush around, to hold our breath, and to miss out on the divine. For many of us, the thought of Christmas may even engender anxiety, disappointment, grief, or anger that leads us to lose sight of the joy, peace, hope, and love that Christ offers us. However, you have chosen to embody this season! You have chosen to savor Advent and explore the contemplative path. You can embrace the waiting with your whole self.

This devotional experience invites you to connect with God this Advent and discover what it means to live life with God. I use the term "with God" to remind myself that every moment is holy and lived with our Creator. You can prepare yourself to spend this time with your Creator. There is no better time than now and you are not alone in the process. You have everything you need to fully experience Advent and the gift of Christmas this season.

Let us enter together into these ponderings, postures, and prayers so that Christmas may be born anew in us. This Advent, may we allow ourselves to be more present with God and fully embody the gifts of this season.

PREPARING FOR CHRISTMAS

"Isn't there anyone who knows what
Christmas is all about?"
—Charlie Brown[1]

Before Jesus' ministry truly began, his cousin John began to preach in the wilderness of Judea. He proclaimed that he was fulfilling the words of the prophet Isaiah who said, "Prepare the way of the Lord, make his paths straight" (Matt. 3:3, NRSV). John knew that Jesus was the Messiah, and he did his part to prepare the way for Jesus and his ministry. This invitation to preparation is still offered to us today.

Admittedly, one of the first things I often prepare each Christmas is not myself; it is my gift list. I enjoy the process of giving creative and thoughtful gifts to my loved ones. Giving is a meaningful tradition to me, but it does not mean I can forget to prepare myself too. The waiting of Advent provides us with the space we need to receive the gift God wants to give us, Christ. Are you preparing the packages and the parties for others alone, or are you also willing to prepare yourself? The season of preparation is a time for opening yourself up to the gift of Christ, and all that gift signifies—hope, peace, joy, and love. The preparation I am inviting you to undertake extends beyond a gift list or a tree. Advent invites us to prepare ourselves by waiting, sensing, and embodying the season.

Whether or not your spiritual journey has led you to embrace this season before, remember that you are not alone in this pursuit. A mentor and friend told me this story of her childhood and it reminds me of the anticipation that comes simply by slowing down and not rushing but instead savoring this season. Hear this story in her words as you recall any of your own Advent (or "preparing for Christmas") memories:

> On the first Sunday of Advent, my mother would gather however many of us five children were born at the time. This always included even the youngest of siblings. We would go into the dining room as she opened a box retrieved from the attic. Although not a surprise, every year, it was a thrill to see inside once more: a wooden manger, about eight inches high and twelve inches long. Mom pulled it out so that each of us could hold it and ask questions. Her answers were always aimed at each child's level of understanding; she wanted us each to be part of the story. Mom then showed us the figurines carefully wrapped in shredded paper, secured by tissue paper and straw, in another box. She would set this aside, telling us we had to wait to see them all, but without fail, different animal figures would come out gradually over the next four weeks. She stressed that the most critical piece was the manger. She set the cradle on the buffet all by itself. She told us that we could look at it every day as we waited for Christmas, that we could think of Baby Jesus who would be there on Christmas morning—because a manger was where he was born. She told us this was more important than the Christmas

tree that would be in our living room or the wreath on our door. This would become our memorable scene. It was like preparing our heart to receive a surprise. We were captivated! Around week two of Advent, a cow would appear, then a sheep in week three. Week four introduced a shepherd way faraway at the end of the buffet table, tending three sheep. On Christmas Eve, Mary and Joseph were found walking toward the manger from the other end of the buffet. Camels were behind them. On Christmas morning, a star appeared atop the manger's straw roof. An angel hovered above on a secret hidden nail. Joseph and Mary were inside the tiny structure now, and a little corn crib sat empty before them. Before presents were ever unwrapped or breakfast prepared on Christmas morning, the youngest child (who could hold a tiny figure) placed Baby Jesus in the crib. The other siblings brought in the shepherds and wise men, even though we were too young to understand they were not there yet. The scene remains with me at age 70 and I recall it each year as Advent begins. I even reconstructed the pageantry when I worked in a nursing home as a chaplain years ago. The residents were able to unfurl the drama in their minds and hearts. Often a person in a wheelchair could be seen exploring the landscape I had constructed. The tiny figures beckoned audiences of all ages. There are myriad ways we wait during Advent, but the empty manger and very absent players seem to have escaped our instant cultural ways. We want it all now! Maybe the emptiness of that hallowed animal stall will give rise to what awaits the longing heart across ages and ages.[2]

The waiting during Advent is a gift we are not to miss, and the best way to avoid missing it is to be present and embody it. To sense it, to live it, to feel it! We can prepare to receive God's gift of Christ with our whole selves as we wait with God for Christmas. That's it. Memories and stories like this one remind us that Christmas is to be anticipated. My friend's mother gave her the simple gift of anticipation each season as she waited for Jesus. She felt that waiting with her whole self; the waiting prepared her for what was to come, the birth of Christ.

We live in a society that offers instant results and quick fixes. But Advent prepares us to receive God's divine gift fully. Are you ready to wait with anticipation as you prepare yourself for Christ this Advent season? What are you waiting for? Take a moment to ponder what it feels like to wait for Christmas. Name it, describe it, draw it, sense it—as you prepare yourself to receive the gift of Christ.

EMBODIMENT AS PRESENCE

"He who attempts to act and do things for others
or for the world without deepening his own self-
understanding, freedom, integrity, and capacity
to love, will not have anything to give others."
—Thomas Merton[1]

Embodiment means that we give life to an idea. It requires that
we take on that idea and personify it in ourselves. In the con-
text of our faith, embodiment means that we give shape to our
thoughts, actions, feelings, and intentions through our physical
self. Embodiment allows us to remain present within ourselves as
we journey through life.[2]

Embodiment can also help shape abstract concepts. God has
promised God's followers many things, and God gives shape to
these promises through the gift of Jesus. We call this gift the
Incarnation, the moment when God became human, in the form
of a baby, and came to live among us. Our Christian faith is pro-
foundly shaped by the Incarnation, by the physical presence of
Jesus Christ in our midst.

In this season of waiting, we prepare to celebrate the gift of
the Incarnation. We prepare to celebrate the birth of Christ. If
not for the embodied gift of the Christ child arriving in that manger, Christmas, as we know it, would not exist. Imagine, for a
moment, Christianity without the birth of the Christ child, without the Incarnation. There would be no life of Christ, no death of

Christ, and most importantly, no resurrection of Christ. As strange as the idea may seem, I cannot imagine it any other way. This is truly a breath-taking realization!

Recently, I attended a retreat with author, teacher, and theologian Dr. Amy Oden. As she shared with us before our time of quiet that day, she talked about embodiment and how the Incarnation of Christ is the ultimate gift to us as Christians. My mind sparked as I listened and remembered how Advent is the time when we prepare to receive this gift. Oden also wrote this about Advent, "Christians believe our bodies are blessed, consecrated by God who became flesh to dwell with us. Our en-flesh-ment connects us to God who meets us where we are, in our bodies, right here."[3]

An embodied Advent invites us to live the experience of this season fully, with our whole selves, right here and right now as we await the Christ child. For many of us, it is challenging to embrace this concept. The world pulls us away from the joy of being present in our bodies and gives us expectations of what our bodies should be, how they should perform, and what they should look like. We forget that our bodies are blessed and consecrated. God did not create the body to bring us doubt or shame. Those emotions are not from God. Instead, God created us as living and breathing human beings who have the ability to live as whole persons— body and spirit together.

To live an embodied life, we must take in all that is around us. In our days of constant busyness, we rarely take the time to be present in our own body. As a result, the body is sometimes the last thing we pay attention to on our daily agenda. Thankfully, recent years have inspired more discussions about bodily awareness. There is nothing like a global pandemic to force us to pay more attention to our bodies, to think about what our bodies are saying and what our bodies need. Such physically challenging times can be a gift. They offer our culture a chance to develop greater awareness of our bodies. We can learn what it looks like to notice and pay attention to our bodies. I have had such an experience; maybe you have too.

In 2005, on Christmas Day, I found myself celebrating the birth of Christ in a hospital rehabilitation room with green and red building blocks scattered across the floor, rather than around a tree with gifts covered in green and red wrapping paper. Earlier that month, on my birthday, I survived a stroke as well as the brain surgery that followed. My recovery was going miraculously well, all things considered. In the wake of such a traumatic health crisis, I was beginning to learn how to walk and dress again.

My parents, in-laws, sister, spouse, and our young son came to sit with me and savor the day. Our family arrived in shifts, with little fanfare, as I was quickly overwhelmed and anxious during my recovery time. Years later, I look at the photos from that day and see my shaved head (a post-craniotomy gift) and a beaming smile of gratitude. My body had been through so much, and yet it was still present to celebrate.

While everyone has not suffered a health crisis like this, most of us carry trauma of some form in our bodies. However, just because we live in wounded bodies does not mean we cannot tap into everything those wounds offer us in order to live more fully present lives with God. In fact, it may be even more acceptable, when wounded, to give ourselves permission to slow down and let go of external expectations.

That Christmas celebration was like none other—it was quiet, simple, slow, and if I'm honest, very dull. Thankfully, our son was too young to notice the lack of entertainment and thrilled to simply be present with his mom. Maybe his example offers us a model for being with God this Advent. Although my body did not allow me to keep up with Christmases past or imagine a more lively Christmas in the future, I was grateful. All I could do was be present in that particular moment with the people I loved most in the world.

That contemplative celebration was my first introduction to slowing down and simply being present in the perfectly imperfect body I had been given. That unexpected culmination of the Advent season came with no expectations, and it has changed the way I savor Advent and enter into Christmas every year since. While celebrations since that day are much more full (and less boring), they remain relatively simple and focused on being present.

That day helped me understand that we can find the gift of Christ inside ourselves. This requires that we willingly let go of external demands and give ourselves permission to be present in whatever situation as we listen to God in our lives. We often try to create picture-perfect moments, but some of my favorite memories are less than perfect. On this less than ideal day, I was present in the perfectly imperfect. Take a moment and think about a memory you cherish for its imperfections. Ponder the gift of this perfectly imperfect moment.

Mary and Joseph lived through a less-than-ideal situation. They each heard God speak, and while confused by what they heard, they listened (see Luke 1:26-35, Matthew 1:18-24). It was not easy, but they did not run away. They followed God's invitation, and because of their willingness to be present with their Creator, we received the gift of Christ. This story is a reminder that we are each perfectly imperfect human beings. We are each given the opportunity to live into this season of waiting. We are each invited to receive the gift of God with us, the gift of Jesus.

God sent Jesus to embody God's presence. While none of us actually know the date of Christ's birth (December 25th was only chosen in the mid 300s), celebrating his arrival during the darkest nights of winter is a perfect symbol for the promises God still makes today.[4] The dark times in my life have allowed me to draw closer to my faith in Christ. God meets us in these dark times. God comes to us and is present with us.

Jesus showed us what it meant to be fully human. He arrived in the dark and lived a full life filled with celebrations, time with friends, gift-giving, and receiving, all without a designated holiday known as Christmas on his calendar. More than anything, Jesus modeled how to stay connected with God. He taught us how to stay in union with the one who created us.

If embodiment and incarnation feel like foreign concepts, let us look not only to the birth but the life of Jesus. The life of Christ offers us guidance. Jesus teaches us to go away and be alone with God to pray (Luke 5:16). Scripture tells us stories of Jesus being present in his body, even to the point of despair, such as in the Garden of Gethsemane when he fell to his knees and sweat drops of blood (Luke 22:39-46). You can indeed look to Jesus today to imagine this connection with God. Consider the story of Jesus being anointed:

> Now while Jesus was at Bethany in the house of Simon the leper, a woman came to him with an alabaster jar of very costly ointment, and she poured it on his head as he sat at the table. But when the disciples saw it, they were angry and said, "Why this waste? For this ointment could have been sold for a large sum, and the money given to the poor." But Jesus, aware of this, said to them, "Why do you trouble the woman? She has performed a good service for me. For you always have the poor with you, but you will not always have me. By pouring this ointment on my body she has prepared me for burial. Truly I tell you, wherever this good news is proclaimed in the whole world, what she has done will be told in remembrance of her."
> —Matthew 26:6-12 (NRSV)

Jesus was clear. The gift of the oil was not a waste. On the contrary, the oil prepared Jesus for what was to come. The experience was preparing his followers. This is a story about preparation and being present with Jesus; this woman was practicing presence and embodying her love of Christ with her gift.

It is humbling to recognize the gift of Christ. It is humbling to acknowledge that God came to us and lived in a body just like ours. When we choose to be present and connect with the gift of the body that we have been given, we can gain an appreciation for the body of Christ and the richness of Advent. If we choose to embody this season of waiting, we are honoring and sharing the ultimate gift we have received as Christians, the Incarnation and life of Christ.

No matter your past Advent experiences, I pray you find your way this season to a deeper, more present, and full life. I pray that your contemplative journey permits you to fully savor this season of waiting with your Creator. May you discover opportunities to anoint special moments and memories that embody Advent in the days ahead.

CONTEMPLATIVE PRACTICES
TO EXPLORE

"Isn't it strange how we cling to the idea that there's
some elusive prayer formula that will revolutionize
our devotional lives, if only we could figure it out?
And of course, we can't figure it out. We rarely trust
what we already know how to do, which is why
we miss many precious encounters with God."
—Claudia Mair Burney[1]

This Advent season, you are invited to discover every single
opportunity to encounter God using a variety of contemplative prayer practices and your very own body. In each daily exercise, you will use your whole self to engage in prayer forms that
are accessible to you, not ones that seem out of reach or elusive.

Contemplative prayer, according to St. Teresa of Avila, "is nothing else than an intimate sharing between friends; it means taking time frequently to be alone with Him who we know loves us."[2]
If you are willing, contemplation can take you into deep places on
your faith journey. You are encouraged to dive in to each practice
as you shift from doing into being and make every aspect of this
Advent season a prayer. Consider these prompts an invitation to
spend time with the one who created you as you wait to celebrate
the birth of Christ.

Each theme of this Advent season—hope, peace, joy, and love—
will have its own chapter and its own week of daily contemplative

exercises. Whether these practices are familiar or new to you, enjoy them in fresh ways this season as you journey through Advent embracing your whole self. What follows is an overview of these practices. Bookmark these pages and refer back to them as needed on your contemplative journey this Advent.

Breath Prayer

Breath prayer is a pivotal practice in my own life, as I shared in my first devotional book, *Holy Listening with Breath, Body, and the Spirit*. A breath prayer is a simple and intimate prayer that can be repeated with each breath, each inhalation and exhalation drawing you nearer to the Spirit of God. I experience breath prayer as an invitation to "pray continually" as Paul writes in 1 Thessalonians 5:17.

I also appreciate the way my body can partake in this kind of prayer with the simple act of breathing. Breath experts, like Donna Farhi in *The Breathing Book,* explain how a simple concept, breathing, affects your entire body, including "your respiratory, cardiovascular, neurological, gastrointestinal, muscular, and psychic systems and also has a general effect on your sleep, your memory, your energy level, and your concentration."[3] Needless to say, breathing is a vital and important aspect of your whole self!

Beyond being physically, mentally, and spiritually beneficial, breath prayer is available to you anytime and anywhere. Each week of our four-week Advent journey includes a breath prayer that you can incorporate into your entire week, not only during your quiet time. You are invited to explore breathwork and breath prayer and embrace how this practice can help you embody hope, joy, peace, and love, while recognizing that God is as close as your next breath.

Practicing Breath Prayer

To allow your breath prayer to become a whole-body experience, I encourage you to take full, deep inhalations and long exhalations as you practice your prayer. There are many ways to practice breathwork, and studies show deep breathing calms the mind. Our bodies are truly magnificent!

In this short overview, I encourage you to explore the fullness of your breath by accessing the depths of your diaphragm. To practice diaphragmatic breathing (also called "belly breathing"), sit tall in a chair, or, if this style of breathing is new to you, you may wish to lie on your back and place one hand on your belly and one on your chest.

Take a few conscious breaths, inhaling and exhaling through your nose, and notice the pause in between each breath. Breathe deeply into your diaphragm and feel your belly expand. Exhale and notice your abdomen contract. Consider the rise and fall of your belly as you breathe while the hand on your chest remains relatively still. Continue your deep breathing as you practice breath prayer for five minutes or more.[4]

Each week, you will be offered an example of a breath prayer in the same format as the one on the following page. If you prefer, feel free to create your own breath prayer by breathing in and out words that draw you closer to the weekly theme and, ultimately, your Creator.

Sample Breath Prayer

Breathe In: A name of God (Lord, Jehovah, El-Shaddai, etc.)
Breathe Out: A longing of your heart (draw me near, prepare me, help me go slow)

Mindful Movement

To embody our spirituality and the gift of incarnation fully, we need to invite our bodies to mindfully participate. Mindfulness invites us to be present in the moment. In *Becoming Safely Embodied*, Deirdre Fay helps us understand how "accepting everything without judgment or reaction" invites us into a more loving state of mind.[5] I think Jesus modeled this acceptance for us. His mindful life on earth did not involve judgment or reaction as he moved about his days. We will use that approach as we choose to mindfully move together.

Throughout this devotional, consider how you can connect with your body in your posture, your movement, and your awareness of the body God created for you, without judgment. Movement is a natural part of who we are as humans, and our bodies move every day in a variety of ways. The body is miraculous and amazing! Mindful movement invites you to discover healing and remain present within yourself.

Mindfulness need not be complicated. As David Emerson, a yoga teacher and trainer who focuses on teaching mindfulness and movement to trauma survivors, writes, "One simple definition of mindfulness is that it is the purposeful direction of attention toward an object (i.e., a sound, a smell, a taste, an emotion, or a body experience."[6] The mindful movement activities in this book are targeted at these responses. You are invited to remain present in each exercise as you become more embodied through mindful movement this Advent.

Practicing Mindful Movement

The mindful movement activities chosen for each week prompt you to do precisely what the name implies—move mindfully (that is, walk, stretch, sing, dance). While the purpose is not exercise, mindfulness can easily be incorporated into your exercise routine if you choose.

Our bodies come in all shapes, sizes, and varying levels of physical ability. These movements are therefore designed to be accessible to all. If your body does not allow for movement in the way described, modify the invitation into a purposeful and meaningful mindfulness exercise that fits your body's needs.

Lectio Divina

The words *lectio divina* are Latin for "holy reading." This ancient prayer practice is composed of four steps: *lectio* ("to read"), *meditatio* ("to reflect"), *oratio* ("to respond"), and *contemplatio* ("to rest"). *Lectio divina* allows you to listen for God using scripture and to connect to God through the ancient Word while delving into a particular passage.

The practice of *lectio divina* focuses on a formational reading of scripture as opposed to an informational reading. Formational reading invites the text to shape you while informational reading invites you to understand the text. Though both types of reading can be useful on a spiritual journey, the art of *lectio divina* allows you to interact with God's Word by meditating on a passage and listening for God to lead you.

If you are new to the practice of *lectio divina*, I have included a brief overview and instructions. Feel free to refer to these instructions until this style of holy reading and meditating on God's Word becomes natural to you. Though the scripture for each week is included in this book in its entirety, you may wish to read the passage in your own Bible or in a different Bible translation. You may also find it helpful to read the scriptures aloud or use an audio Bible or Bible app that reads aloud to you. I encourage you to explore various ways of interacting with God's Word as you practice *lectio divina*.[7]

Practicing Lectio Divina

Prepare for this practice by inviting God to speak to you through a particular passage of scripture as you enjoy being in God's presence. Then, walk through the following four steps one at a time.

1. *Lectio* (Read)—Slowly read or listen to the designated passage one time.
2. *Meditatio* (Reflect)—Read or listen to the passage again. Consider a word, phrase, or image from the passage that draws your attention. Think about what stands out to you. What do you hear, see, or sense? Reflect on how this word, phrase, or image speaks to

you today. Consider repeating your word or phrase silently to yourself.

3. *Oratio* (Respond)—Read or listen to the passage one more time. Respond to what you hear in God's Word and how it makes you feel. Is there an invitation for you in the scripture today? Tell God what you heard or sensed.

4. *Contemplatio* (Rest)—Rest in what you have heard. Receive any clarity, stillness, insight, or imagery that comes to your mind. Give God thanks for this time, and rest in the Word of God.[8]

Visio Divina

While *lectio divina* invites us to pray with scripture, *visio divina* invites us to encounter the divine and pray with images. While this practice of holy gazing is something I had previously participated in many times on retreats, I recently gained a deeper appreciation for the true sensory and embodied nature of the practice.

Remember the wise storyteller who shared about her childhood nativity in the introduction? She came to lead a time of Advent prayer for my small group not long ago. Upon her arrival, she pulled out a lovely piece of fabric, a candle, and a print of a picture depicting Mary and Elizabeth by an artist who was unknown to me at the time, Rev. Lauren Wright Pittman.

As my eyes took in that image, I held my breath and felt my entire body respond. This image captured the essence of Advent for me, the waiting and anticipation. I had no words, just a feeling of God's presence. The artist opened my eyes to much more, both culturally and spiritually, than I had seen before when gazing upon Mary and Elizabeth.

After seeing that image, I began to wonder how we could each embody and discover the gift of the Christ child within ourselves. I contacted the artist and learned that she had dedicated her life to inviting others to engage with God's Word through art. Her works of art are the ones included in this book, and you are invited to use these artworks as you embody the theme of each week through the practice of *visio divina*. If your vision does not allow you to see the art included on these pages, ask a friend to describe it to you in full detail. This will enable you to have your own experience of this artist's magnificent work.

Practicing Visio Divina

As you gaze upon the art, make note of the first color, image, or shape that draws your attention. Allow your gaze to remain steady on this part of the image for a minute or longer as you breathe fully and deeply. Ask yourself what you see.

Next, allow your vision to expand to the full image. Ponder the entire work of art and enjoy this time of contemplation. What do you notice as you expand your gaze? Be present with the art. Breathe deeply and consider the image for another minute or longer.

Once you feel you have absorbed the image in full, ask yourself the following questions:

- What emotions does this art bring forth in you?
- How does this imagery prepare you to receive the gift of Christ this Advent?
- Is there something you see in this artwork that speaks specifically to your life today?
- How does this work of art help you see the theme of the week (hope, peace, joy, or love)?
- Does this art invite you into a deeper form of prayer? If so, how?[8]

After your time of reflection, you may wish to write out your thoughts, offer them to God in prayer, or simply remain silent for a few moments.

Christian Meditation

Christian meditation has been known by many names and practiced in many ways over the ages. Also known as contemplative prayer or centering prayer, many assume that Christian meditation is an exercise in emptying the mind, but that is not quite the case. Instead, Christian meditation invites us into the presence of God while we practice silence. One of my professors and mentors, Dr. Dwight Judy, writes of "the silence of God" and describes contemplative silence by saying that it, "Does not necessarily mean we hear nothing, but rather that in silence we may begin to hear everything."[9] You are encouraged to befriend the silence so you can hear everything this Advent season!

My experience with meditation as a Christian spiritual practice has deepened my relationship with God and my ability to be more present in all that happens in my life. I think of prayer as an opportunity to talk with God. Meditation, on the other hand, is an opportunity to quiet my mind and focus on being with God in the silence.

My own personal meditation practice is based on the concept of centering prayer as passed down in the teachings of Father Thomas Keating.[10] Traditionally, centering prayer is practiced twice a day for approximately twenty to thirty minutes each time. If this type of silent contemplation is new to you, do not be intimidated by that kind of frequency or duration. Allow yourself to start slowly, then increase your time in silence as you become more comfortable. I find it useful to use a sand timer or an app on my phone to keep time.

Meditation is also a physically beneficial practice. Today, meditation is suggested by everyone from physicians to athletes to popular magazines. New scientific findings continue to connect mindfulness and meditation to health and wellness. Mindful practices like meditation help calm our brain's "fight or flight" center, the amygdala, and they are also found to improve both attention span and learning.[11] If you are unsure about meditation from a Christian perspective or are new to the practice, consider reading *One Breath at a Time: A Skeptic's Guide to Christian Meditation* by J. Dana Trent.[12]

But meditation is beneficial beyond its physical advantages. Christian meditation is a beautiful companion to other forms of prayer and a great way to simply "soak in" what God is offering you this season. One of my students called her meditation practice "icing on the cake." Connecting to God through silent meditation makes life a little sweeter. It helps deepen our empathy, grow in our beliefs, and discover a life built on faith in our Creator.

To help you enter into your time of quiet, each meditation exercise will begin with a passage of scripture from the Psalms. You will then be invited to hold the weekly theme as a sacred word in silence before God. Do not be concerned when thoughts and distractions arise. That is to be expected. In these moments, simply repeat your holy word and come back into the presence of God, eventually allowing your sacred word to fall away.

Remember, Christian meditation is not about emptying the mind of all our thoughts but about discovering union with God in the quiet. Thoughts are a normal part of who we are, and while there is no expectation for what you should experience during times of Christian meditation, there is an invitation to yield to the quiet and be present with God. You may wish to sit in silence for as few as three minutes or as long as thirty minutes. It is your decision as you are invited to sit quietly in the presence of God.

Practicing Christian Meditation

Sit in an upright posture with your back supported and hands resting in your lap. Consider setting a timer for however long you choose to meditate.

Read the suggested psalm to center and invite yourself into God's presence.

Allow your eyes to softly close as you bring forth the week's focus word. You are invited to use each week's theme (hope, peace, joy, and love) or practice with your own sacred word if you prefer.

Silently, with your eyes closed, recall your sacred word. Breathe in and out with full, deep breaths. Allow your mind to settle as you allow your word to fade away and your body to become still in God's presence.

When thoughts surface or distractions arise, release them and return to your word and your breathing to draw your focus back to your quiet time with God.

Remain still and breathe for the duration of your time. Offer an "Amen" to close your silent prayer.

Creative Contemplation

There are many ways to contemplate through creativity, but one of my favorites is writing poetry. You do not need any experience to explore the style of poetry we will use in this book. All you need is a willingness to be creative and an open mind to write your acrostic poem each week.

An acrostic poem uses all the letters in a word or name as the first letter of each line of the poem. The acrostic poem can rhyme, but that is not required. There is no right or wrong way to create this poem. If you enjoy other styles of poetry, consider writing a poem in a different format to help you reflect and draw you nearer to God.

Each acrostic poem will include space for you to write a poem of your own, as well as an example of a poem that you can use to draw inspiration.

Practicing Presence

Brother Lawrence, a lay monk in the seventeenth century, wrote, "I cannot imagine how religious persons can live satisfied without the practice of the presence of God."[13] Each week during this Advent season, you'll be presented with a final exercise to help you practice presence. This is an opportunity to use your body, your breath, and your senses to be present in every moment as you wait for the birth of Christ and the Incarnation.

While presence is a simple concept to explain, it is a challenging concept to embrace. During this Advent journey, experience these moments of presence with your whole self and notice how practicing presence each week invites you to be more present throughout your day. This is not a time of silent meditation, although it may be quiet. It is a chance to simply be present with the activity and therefore more comfortable with practicing presence in your everyday life.

Remember that this whole season is about waiting with anticipation for the presence of God in Jesus. It is about waiting for Emmanuel, God with us. Hear this from the psalmist and be reminded that God is near in this time of Advent:

Where can I go from your spirit?
    Or where can I flee from your presence?
If I ascend to heaven, you are there;
    if I make my bed in Sheol, you are there.
If I take the wings of the morning
    and settle at the farthest limits of the sea,
even there your hand shall lead me,
    and your right hand shall hold me fast.

If I say, "Surely the darkness shall cover me,
    and night wraps itself around me,"
even the darkness is not dark to you;
    the night is as bright as the day,
    for darkness is as light to you.
—Psalm 139:7-12 (NRSV)

Take advantage of this often cold and dark season full of waiting and anticipation to practice presence and discover a new satisfaction in your relationship with God. Allow these contemplative practices to help you not miss a moment with God during this waiting season. Allow God to be your light as you embrace the fullness of your humanity and encounter the fullness of God's divine nature.

Practicing Presence

Read the mindfulness activity and invitation to practice presence and follow the prompts to engage your body and spirit (that is, use your senses, eat mindfully, practice a body scan, etc.).

HOW TO USE THIS
DEVOTIONAL

"We want to go to God for answers, but
sometimes what we get is God's presence."
—Nadia Bolz-Weber[1]

This devotional is an invitation to experience an embodied Advent. But let me be clear that there is no recipe for a perfect experience, nor is there any expectation for what you should (or should not) hear from God during your times of contemplation, prayer, and meditation. Each person's experience will be different.

Nevertheless, everyone can experience the entire presence of God in this season. Everyone can prepare the whole self to welcome the gift of Christ. I invite you to fully embrace this opportunity to be in God's presence, this opportunity to anticipate God's presence. Any experience beyond that is your gift from God.

This book is also designed to be accessible and approachable. Think about it more like a retreat than a book you pick up and put back down when you're done reading. The daily practices offer an overview of various ways to meet God in your own life each day. You can spend a few minutes a day on each exercise to cultivate presence in this season, or if time allows, dig deeper and soak in extended time of contemplation. Allow yourself to spend as much time as you are able each day without feeling burdened. The point of all this is to be encouraged by the opportunity to be with God.

From a few minutes to a few hours, each of these exercises can be experienced at your pace.

Prayer, mindfulness, and meditation are embodied practices that have been shown to help us remain more present, reduce anxiety, decrease stress, and improve our overall health. In a season that can often become stressful and overwhelming, these practices invite you to care for the body God created. Allow your day to be transformed by these contemplative exercises and by purposeful presence this Advent season.

These practices invite you to not only care for yourself but to be more present with your loved ones. Consider this, when you are more grounded, present, and connected within yourself, you have greater capacity to be available for those around you. We have all experienced that moment when we realize we have not heard a word our partner, friend, or child has spoken to us. Even though our bodies may appear present, our minds are not. These embodied practices will not only improve your connection between body and spirit, they can help you be in better relationships with those you love simply by being more present in your daily life.

In my work as a trained spiritual director and yoga instructor, I've noticed that we are the ones who tend to complicate our relationship with God and make it harder than it needs to be. We are the ones who create false expectations about what we should be experiencing, about what our bodies should be feeling.

But the contemplative experience is not a legalistic one. It is not rigid. It is an opportunity to connect with God in the here and now. Try to avoid comparing your spiritual life or your body to anyone else's. With a practice of presence, we may or may not find answers to our questions, but we can seek to discover God in every moment of this season and every season.

Think of this time of contemplation as a gift you are giving yourself, one that continues to provide beyond the daily quiet time. You will use tools and develop practices in the days to come that can give back to your body and spirit long after you get up from your quiet place or after the Christmas season ends. You will foster time with God that is personal. Allow this time to be one you cultivate for yourself and claim the time you need in this season to develop your inner and embodied life with God.

Remember that this is your personal experience. Use the designated journaling space or the margins of the book to note moments of resistance as well as moments of clarity. If you don't consider yourself a journaler, simply jot down words and phrases that come to mind. Draw doodles or sketch images that bring you back to what you may have noticed, heard, or felt. These moments of clarity may or may not be related to Advent or even to God at all. Notice what rises up and ask God to show you what it means.

While spiritual embodiment is an individual experience, our spiritual formation often takes shape when we process or share our experience with others. Therefore, beyond the time you spend following these practices, beyond the time of meditation and reflection and journaling, consider inviting a friend to join you on this embodiment journey so that you can share what you hear, notice, and learn along the way. If journeying alone, consider sharing or processing your experience with a spiritual director or small group during this season (see the small-group guide in the back of this book). You might even consider returning to this book in future Advent seasons to share your growth with yourself!

CREATE PURPOSEFUL SPACE

I always put the Lord in front of me;
I will not stumble because he is on my right side.
That's why my heart celebrates and my mood is joyous;
yes, my whole body will rest in safety.
—Psalm 16:8-9 (CEB)

Having a designated space to be present with God allows us to be more present. Noise, people, and clutter, both in our minds and our physical space, can be distracting and overwhelming. While you do not need a perfect space to meet God (the manger, for instance, was not ideal), I urge you to find a place where you can be purposefully present this Advent season. Choose a set area for your time apart—even if it is in your closet!

At home, I have a couple spaces set apart for embodied presence and prayer. This allows me to slip away to one or the other when family members are also in the house. One prayer space is in my bedroom on my yoga mat. I roll this up daily or else our dog decides to take residence there—another challenge for quiet time at home.

The other space is on the couch in the den. I have a portable tray dedicated to unique items that help keep me grounded and present in my prayer time. My tray includes Jesus icons, prayer beads, a hand cross, prayer stones, scripture cards, essential oils, and more. On a shelf nearby, I store a prayer shawl that was given to me when my dad passed away, as well as my Bibles, a journal, and colored pencils. Additionally, during the Advent season, I always keep an Advent wreath for our family to enjoy.

Consider making your own Advent altar or prayer tray for this contemplative prayer journey. The color blue is often used to signify the waiting and hope of the Advent season. You may wish to incorporate that hopeful color in your set up in some way, perhaps a blue piece of cloth or a blue ribbon. Candles are also a traditional part of Advent wreaths. Use one single candle or up to four candles to represent the four weeks we will embody together. You can even place a nativity ornament or empty cradle in your space as a reminder of what we are anticipating together. Focus your prayer station on the embodied waiting of Advent and the coming of Christ.

In addition to creating a physical space, it is also vital to create purposeful space in your schedule and set aside time for prayer. While I do not consider myself a morning person, I know that my days go better when I begin my morning in prayer. You may decide to set aside a few moments each morning to practice the day's exercise then return later in the day, or you may choose to close your day with your prayers and reflections. No matter when you decide is best, choose to claim this time with God.

I am often asked how I find time to use every prayer tool during my daily prayers. The answer is quite simple: I don't! When I become present with God, I reach into my toolbox to find what God draws me to that day. Some days I am drawn to time on my yoga mat or with my prayer beads. In the same way that you don't use the same tool when building a house, we should not use the same tool for building and shaping our souls. This type of work requires a complete toolbox that gives us options and allows us to use what we need for the time required.

As you explore the exercise and prompts in this book, you may find some tools that resonate with you more than others, and that is exactly as it should be. I invite you to experience and use all the tools at first. You never know when you may reach for one now or in the future. But ultimately you should use what works best for you. Be sure to pay attention to any resistance you feel during any of the exercises and ask God to show you how that resistance can help make you more present. This is a practice of embodiment. Most importantly, remember that the practice of prayer and contemplation is not about the tools we use; it is about purposefully entering God's presence.

As the psalmist writes in Psalm 16, when we meet God, our whole body rests in safety. Our world overflows with distractions. Setting apart a time and place where you feel equipped to meet God is vital in this embodied Advent journey. Before you read any further, prepare yourself to meet God on purpose and consider where and when you will meet God each day.

Slow Down and Hope

I hope, LORD.
My whole being hopes,
and I wait for God's promise.
—Psalm 130:5 (CEB)

Let us begin our embodiment journey by slowing down and focusing on the theme of hope. Ponder the word "hope" for a moment. It is a feeling of expectation. It is a desire for a certain thing to happen. Hope comes first in our journey because hope forms the basis for this season of anticipation. What does hope look like to you? Pause and reflect on this question. If it helps, take a moment to write out your thoughts. What are you hoping for this Advent?

In Psalm 130:5, the psalmist puts into words the all-encompassing nature of hope. Hope can fill our whole being if we allow it. Now, consider another word the psalmist uses in this same verse: wait. The Advent season is about hope, but it is also about waiting. Over these four weeks, we are waiting together for the promise of Christ to arrive.

This time that we spend waiting also provides us with the opportunity to prepare for the things that we hope for. You are reading this book because you want to prepare yourself this season. You want to prepare yourself for the arrival of the Christ child. It matters to you.

You may long to have a more embodied faith. Perhaps you're in search of companionship and guidance on your journey of faith. Maybe you just want to be inspired to discover something new and fresh this Advent. Maybe after all the struggles you have faced in your life, you are not sure how to kindle hope within yourself and are longing for these embodied practices to help you.

No matter where you are on your faith journey, no matter what has brought you here during this Advent season, remember that these practices are not meant to be a chore. Practicing presence through prayer should give you life. Meditation should give you life. Mindfulness, journaling, and breathwork should give you life. During this time, God invites you to be more present and aware of the hope God offers you this season. This journey is about opening yourself up to that invitation.

Take a moment to process the invitation God is offering you and choose one way that you will prioritize yourself this Advent season and ignite your hope. You could choose anything from setting aside time for quiet prayer to focusing on your physical movement to being intentional about the foods you choose to fuel your body. Perhaps you want to pay closer attention to your relationships with others or center your spiritual connection with God. Whatever you choose, spend a moment considering how you will make this a priority. Think about how your choice will offer you hope in Christ and in life this Advent season.

As you define your priorities, remember the words of the psalmist in Psalm 130:5. Whether the concept of embodiment is new to you or something you've practiced for years, consider how your whole being can hope for something. If we allow our bodies to be the home for our spiritual longings, then we are embracing embodied spirituality. If we choose to embrace embodied spirituality, we are reflecting our spirituality not simply with our words, but with our whole selves.

Do you long to embody hope this season? Do you need hope now more than ever before? Are you longing to truly feel hope with your whole self?

Close your eyes and ask yourself: Where do you feel hope in your body? Many of us connect to hope with our heart or our gut. Maybe hope to you is more about reason and thought, and you feel it in your head. Maybe for you hope is about doing something, and you feel it in your hands and your feet. Think about where you feel hope. Take a few breaths and try to connect with where you feel it inside yourself. Then, place a hand on that part of your body and breathe. If you are struggling to connect hope with a physical part of yourself, simply place a hand over your heart and ask God for hope as you breathe.

When you are ready to move on, ask yourself if there is a part of you that is holding back from feeling hope, perhaps even to protect you. It's not uncommon for us to put up walls to avoid disappointment. This is a normal response. However, I invite you to think about what it would look like to hope with your entire being. What would it mean?

As a Christian, you already know the end of the Advent story. Christ is coming! Not "Christ might come," or "Christ will get around to coming eventually," but "Christ *is* coming." The gift of Christ is the physical symbol of our hope in human form. Christ is God with us.

Throughout this week of Advent, the spiritual practices found in this book invite you to wait with God and practice cultivating hope in your physical form. Some of the daily practices may seem simple, but practicing presence with God need not be complicated. The hardest part for most of us when cultivating contemplation is carving out the time to be with God and wait.

My hope for you this Advent season is that you create the space to live an embodied life that will fill you to overflowing with the hope of Christ.

Let us prepare ourselves as we wait together. Your invitation this week is to slow down long enough to explore hope using the spiritual practices offered. If you begin to feel worried or concerned about slowing down, take a breath and process those emotions. Pause wherever you are and make space to simply wait with God before moving on to the next exercise.

Christ comes to us as a gift. Let us not be too busy to notice. Instead, let us slow down and hope!

Journal Prompt for Week 1

Write about or draw an image of something you are hoping for this Advent season. Write down any insights or clarity you received from the opening words for this week. Consider sharing these insights and your thoughts on hope with a spiritual friend or small-group companion.

Opening Prayer for Week 1

Creator God, help me slow down and find your hope. Allow me to connect more deeply with my hopes as I receive the hope you have promised us through the gift of Christ this season. Amen.

DAILY PRACTICES FOR WEEK 1

Slow Down and Hope

Use any or all of this week's daily practices to help you slow down and hope. Consider gathering items that offer you hope this week and either place them on a prayer altar or tape them in this book. Return to them as you work through these practices.

Day 1: Breath Prayer—Hope

Your breath is always with you. It is not something that we choose to do and then set aside as we go about our day. This constant presence makes breath prayer one of my favorite ways to connect with God. Just like your breath, God is always with you!

Explore your breath as a form of prayer today. Connect with the breath in your body by finding a comfortable posture (seated or reclined) and take full, deep breaths filling your diaphragm, then exhale completely. Place one hand on your heart and your other hand on your belly.

> As you breathe in, expand your belly and say to
> yourself: Creator
> As you breathe out, deflate your belly and say to
> yourself: give me hope

Connect your inhale and exhale as well as your
words, offering your simple breath prayer to God.

Repeat this prayer for five to ten minutes.

Inhale: Creator
Exhale: give me hope

Ponder and Go Forth

- How does slowing down for breath prayer invite you to embody this week's theme of hope?
- Notice how your body feels after five to ten minutes of purposeful breathing and praying. Share what you notice in your body and your spirit with a friend or your small group.
- As you go about your day, breathe in and out purposefully, embodying God's gift of hope. Practice your breath prayer in the car, at your desk, or while waiting in line at the grocery store.

Day 2: Mindful Movement—Walk in Hope

In the winter, movement becomes a challenge for me, especially as I age. While I love the outdoors and remain committed to daily walks with our family dog, I often bundle up and simply try to check it off my list during the colder months. Unfortunately, this leaves little space for slow wandering and pondering. Nevertheless, mindful movement is vital to slowing down, even in winter. This mindful walking meditation requires little space, is not dependent on the weather, and invites you to be present wherever you may find yourself.

Hopeful Steps: A Walking Meditation

You can practice walking meditation either indoors or outside. For this mindfulness exercise, you need only ten to fifteen feet of space. Consider walking inside your home, in your yard, or around your neighborhood.

First, pause and bring awareness to your breath with several full, deep rounds of inhaling and exhaling. Close your eyes to feel your body standing tall and grounded. Ask God to fill your steps with hope today.

With your eyes open, place one foot in front of the other. Notice as each foot touches the ground. Pay attention when you lift your foot, feeling the bottom of your foot lift off the earth. Continue moving forward slowly and purposefully with each step.

It may be helpful to say, "I am stepping in hope" to yourself as you mindfully walk. This is a practice that requires focus, and the repetition of this phrase helps keep you present and connects you with your purpose.

As you walk, notice the sound of your breath, the rhythm of your heart, and the way it feels to go slowly on purpose.

After walking a set distance, turn around and notice your body as it adjusts to the turn. Again, walk slowly and purposefully in hope. Walk for as long as you wish, staying present in your hopeful steps.

Once you have completed your walking meditation, stand still and notice any sensations or shifts in your body and spirit as you give thanks to God for hope. Then, carry this hope with you in your steps as you move into the remainder of your day.

Ponder and Go Forth

- How can you invite God to fill your steps with hope this season?
- Is it challenging to go slowly on purpose? Why?
- How will you carry these steps of hope into today and into the days to come?
- How else might you incorporate mindful walking into your day?

Day 3: Lectio Divina—Hear Hope

Scripture invites us to connect with God's Word. As you pause today to reflect on a passage you have likely read before, choose to open yourself to hear it with fresh ears. Prepare yourself to listen by inviting God to speak to you through the scripture.

Settle in and read Matthew 1:22-23 slowly, in *lectio divina* style. If listening to an audio recording of the scripture, consider sitting tall in a chair or finding a seated meditation pose.

Today's Scripture

Look! A virgin will become pregnant and give birth to a son,
And they will call him, Emmanuel.
(Emmanuel means "God with us.")
—Matthew 1:22-23 (CEB)

Lectio (Read)—Slowly read or listen to Matthew 1:22-23 one time.

Meditatio (Reflect)—Read or listen to the passage again. Consider a word, phrase, or image from the passage that draws your attention. What stands out to you? Give birth? Emmanuel? God with us? What do you hear, see, or sense? Reflect on how the word, phrase, or image you chose speaks to you today. Repeat your word or phrase silently to yourself.

Oratio (Respond)—Read or listen to the scripture again. Respond to what you hear God saying in this first chapter of Matthew. How does it makes you feel? What invitation do you see in this scripture for your breath, body, or spirit? Tell God what you heard or sensed.

Contemplatio (Rest)—Rest in what you have heard. Receive any clarity, stillness, insight, or imagery that comes to mind.

Ponder and Go Forth

- Reflect on any glimpses of hope this passage offers you through the promise of Emmanuel.
- What does the name Emmanuel evoke in you? Do you sense God is with you today?
- What is God's invitation for you this Advent?
- How might you rest in what this scripture offers you today?

Day 4: Visio Divina—See Hope

No two people ever experience the practice of *visio divina* in the same way. You and I may each be drawn to different elements of a piece of artwork. But no matter what draws our attention, we find hope in the fact that we are willing to pause and notice. There is always more to be seen, more to discover, and more to offer on this journey of life.

Look at the picture of the magi, titled *The Wisemen's Dream*, on the following page. As you look at this picture, note the first thing that gains your attention. Is there a color, image, or aspect of the artwork that draws your eye? Keep your gaze steady on this part of the image for a minute or longer and breathe fully and deeply. What do you see now? Consider the sleeping travelers. Notice the long windy road. Pay attention to the hand pointing the way.

Let your vision expand to the full image. Soak in the entire work of art and enjoy this time of contemplation. What else do you notice? Continue breathing fully and deeply as you reflect for another few minutes until you have absorbed the fullness of the art.

Take some time to respond to the following questions:

- What emotion does this artwork bring forth in you?
- How does this image prepare you to receive the gift of Christ this Advent season?
- What do you see in this artwork that speaks to your life today?

- How does this image help you see the invitation of hope?
- Does this experience invite you into a deeper form of prayer? If so, how?

You may wish to journal about your reflections, offer them to God in prayer, or simply remain silent for a few minutes.

Ponder and Go Forth

- Imagine the wise men and their long journey. What do you think they hoped for along the way?
- What journey are you on with God? What are your hopes?
- Do you see their fatigue? How does their journey resonate with yours?
- Notice the hand guiding them. Who or what shows you the way this Advent?

Day 5: Christian Meditation—Sit in Hope

If meditation is new to you, then it can feel uncomfortable. This is normal. Whether Christian meditation is new to you or a familiar favorite, give yourself permission to sit today with the idea that your whole being can be a vessel for hope.

Sit in an upright posture with your back supported and hands resting in your lap. If you desire, set a timer for the length of time you want to meditate. If you are new to meditation or if you feel out of practice, start with just a few minutes of silence.

Read Psalm 130:5 to center yourself and accept the invitation into God's presence.

I hope, LORD.
My whole being hopes,
    and I wait for God's promise.
—Psalm 130:5 (CEB)

Allow your eyes to close softly as you bring forth the word "hope" or the sacred word of your choosing.

Silently, with your eyes remaining closed, continue to repeat your sacred word. Breathe in and out with full, deep breaths. Let your mind settle as you allow your word to fade away and your body to become still in God's presence.

When thoughts surface or distractions arise, release them and return to your word. Let the repetition of that word draw your focus back to your quiet time with God.

Remain still and breathe for the duration of your time with God.

Offer an "amen" to close your silent prayer.

Ponder and Go Forth

- Whether or not you have practiced silent prayer or Christian meditation before, notice how it feels today.
- Does the quiet fill you with hope? Is it challenging to still your mind? Is it welcome?
- How does your body feel after completing this type of quiet contemplation? How will you choose to embrace a silent form of prayer and meet God in this season?

Day 6: Creative Contemplation—Write Hope

Pick up a pen, pencil, or crayon and use the space provided below to create an acrostic poem using the word "hope." An acrostic poem uses all the letters in a word as the first letter of each line of the poem. The acrostic poem may rhyme, but it does not need to. There is no right or wrong way to create this poem. There are no expectations for what arises. Instead, simply make space to see what God brings up with the prompt below.

Take a few deep breaths to boost your creativity, then ponder the ways you have experienced hope this week. Consider how you desire to slow down and hope during this Advent season.

Fill in your poem below:

H

O

P

E

Use the following example if you need more inspiration.

Holding onto things that
Overwhelm takes me away from God
Purposefully slowing down and breathing in God's presence
Evokes hope in my soul this season

Ponder and Go Forth

- Did the words that surfaced in your poem about hope surprise you? Why?
- Is your poem also a prayer? How can you make use of it in the future?

Day 7: Practicing Presence—Sense Hope

Through the daily practices this week, you have connected with your breath, listened to scripture with your ears, used your eyes to see God's invitation, allowed your mind to rest in the presence of our Creator, and created something new from your contemplations. All the while, you have been slowing down and cultivating hope.

As we close week one, I invite you into a posture of presence. Practicing presence in everyday life should not feel intimidating. I often use this practice myself, especially during overwhelming or anxious times.[1] Engaging your body in prayer is powerful and helps you draw nearer to God's presence. It allows you to receive the hope we have worked on cultivating this week.

Use today's practice to find your presence in any situation. This exercise could even be explored outdoors at night under the stars for a deeper connection to the wise men and their journey in search of God.

Find a comfortable seated posture, indoors or outside. This exercise is an opportunity to use your five senses to practice mindfulness quickly in any situation. For everyone from children to adults, it's an easy way to practice presence. You may even consider inviting loved ones into this practice with you this week. If any one of the senses used in this activity is not accessible to you, cling to the senses that are accessible and focus on those. Allow any thoughts that arise about concerns outside of this activity to simply be released without judgment and return to the exercise.

- Notice five things you can see. Look around and bring your attention to five things that you can see around you. Try to notice five things in minute detail (examples: the twinkling of the stars, the pattern or color of your clothes, the light or shadows around you, and so forth).
- Notice four things you can feel. With your sense of touch, notice four things you can feel (examples: this book in your hands, your shirt or pants, your own skin, and so forth).
- Notice three things you can hear. Quiet yourself and notice three things you can hear (Examples: the wind blowing, the sounds of an appliance, cars passing by, and so forth).
- Notice two things you can smell. Breathe in and notice two things you smell—pleasant or unpleasant (Examples: your shampoo, a candle burning, the trash, and so forth).
- Notice one thing you can taste. Finally, notice one thing you taste. Or, take a moment now to taste something delicious (Examples: tea, coffee, and so forth).

Ponder and Go Forth

- What did you notice that you did not expect to notice?
- How does becoming present in your body and in your surroundings give you hope when you feel overwhelmed?
- Does practicing presence help you feel less overwhelmed? Why or why not?
- Consider how the simplicity of practicing presence allows you to slow down and make space for more hope this week.

Closing Prayer for Week 1

Creator God, thank you for creating my whole self. Help me to continue to slow down and hope, be mindful and present, and use my body to draw closer to you on the journey this Advent. Make me a wise one who seeks you always. Amen.

Simplify for Peace

Let the LORD give strength to his people!
Let the LORD bless his people with peace!
—Psalm 29:11 (CEB)

You are the Lord's people! The Lord longs to bless you with peace! The scriptures and prayer practices chosen for this week invite you to lean into peace as you meet God in your prayer space. To prepare yourself for this invitation, I want you to simplify this week. Simplify at one of the busiest times of the year? Yes, simplify indeed.

Think about what "simplify" means to you. You may have instantly thought about some part of your life that feels overwhelming, some task or responsibility that requires all of your energy just to manage. This invitation is not a call to fix those things that overwhelm you. That would be overwhelming all by itself. Instead, take a moment to ponder one way you can simplify your life. Choose just one aspect of your life that you can make a little bit simpler. If you need a nudge, consider these ideas:

- Clear that pile of papers from your desk.
- Allow someone else to take over a task at home or work.
- Choose to wear fewer outfits (less laundry to wash).

- Delete a distracting social media app or game from your phone.
- Decide to give fewer gifts (and therefore wrap fewer gifts).
- Send fewer Christmas cards, or none at all.
- Pass on the extra decorations you never use to someone who could use them.

What one part of your life will you find the strength to release this week so you can make more space to receive the gift of peace? It can be big or small. Whatever you choose, it is enough. We often place lots of expectations on ourselves as Christians. Consider how letting go of these expectations could simplify your routine, your Advent season, and your life and allow you to discover more peace.

Psalm 29:11 invites us to both strength and peace. We use God's strength to keep going in challenging times, and the peace we find in those times comes from God as well. There is a magnet on my refrigerator with an anonymous quote. You may have seen it before. It reads, "Peace. It does not mean to be in a place where there is no noise, trouble, or hard work. It means to be in the midst of those things and still be calm in your heart." I believe God is the way we find that kind of peace, and it is a peace that passes all understanding (Philippians 4:6).

Peace can feel like an impossible goal without God. After all, world peace, peace among neighbors, or even a bit of peace on social media is tough to find these days. Politics, blatant acts of racism, a pandemic, and more have left us weary. Instead of focusing on the tumultuous nature of the world, this week you are invited to start from within and discover that place of calm in your heart amidst all life's challenges. The Lord offers peace, and that is a gift for each of us to receive this Advent.

Once you have decided how you will simplify, contemplate ways to purposefully cultivate peace within yourself this week. Consider the following options:

- Turn off the television and turn on a peaceful playlist.
- Choose to go into your prayer space when you begin to feel overwhelmed and take deep purposeful breaths.
- Offer kindness to a stranger and notice how that gives you peace.

Last week you began, or perhaps reignited, a habit of slowing down in daily life and setting aside time for daily contemplative practices. You may have noticed that slowing down can reveal the overwhelming parts of your life. Slowing down can help you see ways that you have become distracted or less present in your life. Slowing down can also show you where you lack peace in life. It is challenging to slow down and simplify. It is hard to simplify when your mind is full of clutter. This week's practices invite you to recognize the benefits of contemplative prayer and make space in your life and in your mind. Do not be weary. Let us simplify and practice together receiving the gift of God's peace.

Journal Prompt for Week 2

Let us make room for peace! Write a sentence or sketch an image about one way you will choose to simplify and make room for peace this week. Consider sharing this with a spiritual friend or small-group companion.

Opening Prayer for Week 2

Creator God, help me simplify and find your peace in the everyday moments of my life. Amen.

DAILY PRACTICES FOR WEEK 2

Simplify for Peace

Use any or all of this week's daily practices to simplify for peace. Consider gathering items that bring you peace this week and either place them on a prayer altar or tape them in this book. Return to them as you work through these practices.

Day 1: Breath Prayer—Peace

As you get more comfortable practicing your breathwork this week, see if you can lengthen your exhalations, feeling the peace that deep breaths offer your body and spirit. Connect with the breath in your body by finding a comfortable posture (seated or reclined) and take full, deep breaths filling your diaphragm, then exhale completely. Place one hand on your heart and your other hand on your belly.

As you breathe in, expand your belly and say to
yourself: Spirit
As you breathe out, deflate your belly and say to
yourself: fill me with peace
Connect your inhale and exhale as well as your
words, offering your simple breath prayer to God.

Repeat this prayer for five to ten minutes.

Inhale: Spirit
Exhale: fill me with peace

Ponder and Go Forth

- Your body responds to simple breathing exercises. Notice how this simple prayer offers you a few moments of peace.
- Journal or share what you notice in your body and your spirit with a friend or your small group.
- As you go about your day, breathe in and out purposefully, embodying God's gift of peace.

Day 2: Mindful Movement—Stretch in Peace

After my health crisis, regularly practicing yoga eased my chronic pain and helped calm my anxious mind. For this reason, I am passionate about inviting others into various types of mindful movement. A practice such as yoga can help the body recover through gentle stretching and exercise, and it helps the mind as it learns to remain present in each posture.

If you are new to the practice of yoga, consider this a time of stretching. It is not necessary to be a regular yoga practitioner to reap the physical benefits of the practice. However, if you are an experienced yoga practitioner, use the exercise below as a warmup, then set peace as the intention of your more extended yoga practice today.

Find a place to rest on the floor and use a yoga mat if you have one accessible. If the floor is not accessible, practice this stretch while lying in your bed.

Reach your arms wide and spread your legs to the edges of your mat to form the shape of a star. As you extend your limbs in the star shape, reach through your hands and feet, then take a full breath in through your nose.

Next, draw your knees into your chest as you exhale fully. You may wish to hug your knees as you pull them into your body.

Move between these two poses as you breathe deeply, shifting your body from the five-pointed star position then bringing your knees to your chest repeatedly for several minutes. As you move and breathe, ask God to fill your body with peace.

Ponder and Go Forth

- Do you feel at peace with your body? How can you invite God to fill your body with peace this season?
- How can your body's movements become a prayer? How can your body speak to God when you lack the words you wish to say?
- How might you carry this sense of peace with you as you carry on with your day?

Day 3: Lectio Divina—Hear Peace

When someone warns you not to be afraid, the natural reaction is to be a little frightened! But today's message arrives from an angel, and it is filled with peace. Prepare yourself to listen by inviting God to speak to you through the scripture.

Settle in and read Luke 2:10-14 slowly, in *lectio divina* style. If listening to an audio recording of the scripture, consider sitting tall in a chair or finding a seated meditation pose.

Today's Scripture

The angel said, "Don't be afraid! Look! I bring good news to you—wonderful, joyous news for all people. Your savior is born today in David's city. He is Christ the Lord. This is a sign for you: you will find a newborn baby wrapped snugly and lying in a manger." Suddenly a great assembly of the heavenly forces was with the angel praising God. They said, "Glory to God in heaven, and on earth peace among those whom he favors."
—Luke 2:10-14 (CEB)

Lectio (Read)—Slowly read or listen to Luke 2:10-14 one time.

Meditatio (Reflect)—Read or listen to the passage again. Consider a word, phrase, or image from the passage that draws your attention. Think about what stands out to you. Don't be afraid? Your savior is born? Peace among those whom he favors? What do you hear, see, or sense? Reflect on how the word, phrase, or image you chose speaks to you today. Repeat your word or phrase silently to yourself.

Oratio (Respond)—Read or listen to the passage one more time. Respond to what you hear in God's Word and how it makes you feel. Is there an invitation of peace for you in the scripture today? Tell God what you heard or sensed.

Contemplatio (Rest)—Rest in what you have heard. Receive any clarity, stillness, insight, or imagery that comes to your mind. Give God thanks for this time and rest in the Word of God.

Ponder and Go Forth

- Reflect on any glimpses of peace this passage offers you through the words of the angel.
- What does the promise of Christ's coming evoke in you?
- How might you rest in what this scripture provides you as you prepare to celebrate the birth of Jesus?
- Consider one way you have experienced God's peace for yourself. You may quickly find that your inner peace begins to spread to your loved ones and your neighbors.

Day 4: Visio Divina—See Peace

Gaze upon this artistic interpretation of the holy family, titled *Ordinary Glory*, found on the following page. As you look at this image, note the first thing that draws your attention. Is there a color, image, or other aspect of the artwork that gains your attention first? Keep your gaze steady on this part of the image for a minute or longer while breathing fully and

deeply. What do you see now? Do you see a yawning Jesus? Notice the star. Observe the faces.

Let your vision expand to the full image. Soak in the entire work of art and enjoy this time of contemplation. What else do you notice? Continue breathing fully and deeply as you reflect for another few minutes until you have absorbed the fullness of the art.

Take some time to respond to the following questions:

- What emotion does this artwork bring forth in you?
- How does this image prepare you to receive the gift of Christ this Advent season?
- What do you see in this artwork that speaks to your life today?
- How does this image help you see the invitation to peace?
- Does this experience invite you into a deeper form of prayer? If so, how?
- You may wish to journal about your reflections, offer them to God in prayer, or simply remain silent for a few minutes.

Ponder and Go Forth

- Does the image of the Messiah as a baby seem complex or straightforward to you? Why?
- What do you notice about the faces of Mary, Joseph, and Jesus in this scene?
- What shapes or elements of this image invite you to embrace the week's theme of simplifying for peace?

- Examine the repeated images in the space surrounding the holy family. What do you see?
- Notice the star. Step outside in God's creation tonight and use your imagination to soak in this scene.

Day 5: Christian Meditation—Sit in Peace

Silence offers peace when we allow our minds to join the quiet and not just our bodies. Settle into your body as you sit in an upright posture with your back supported and hands resting in your lap. If you choose, set a timer for however long you want to meditate.

Read Psalm 29:11 to center yourself and accept the invitation into God's presence.

Let the Lord give strength to his people!
Let the Lord bless his people with peace!
—Psalm 29:11 (CEB)

Allow your eyes to close softly as you bring forth the word "peace" or another sacred word of your choosing.

Silently, with your eyes remaining closed, continue to repeat your sacred word. Breathe in and out with full, deep breaths. Let your mind settle as you allow your word to fade away and your body to become still in God's presence.

When thoughts surface or distractions arise, release them and return to your word. Let the repetition of that word draw your focus back to your quiet time with God.

Remain still and breathe deeply for the duration of your time with God.

Offer an amen to close your silent prayer.

Ponder and Go Forth

- Does sitting in silence with God bring peace to your body and spirit? Why or why not?
- How do your body and spirit feel after completing this type of contemplation?
- How can you practice simplifying your prayer life in this season by savoring silence?

Day 6: Creative Contemplation—Write Peace

Pick up a pen, pencil, or crayon and use the space provided below to create an acrostic poem using the word "peace." Remember, this is an exercise to see what rises up in your time of creativity. There is no right or wrong answer.

Take a few deep breaths to boost your creativity, then ponder the ways you have experienced peace this week. Consider how you have already chosen to simplify for peace during this Advent season.

Fill in your poem below:

P

E

A

C

E

Use the following example if you need more inspiration.

Purposefully
Exploring
All aspects of
Creation helps me
Experience peace

Ponder and Go Forth

- What does God want you to notice about your poem?
- Are there other ways you could be creative with God this week and cultivate more peace?

Day 7: Practicing Presence—Sense Peace

Through the daily practices this week, you have been invited to simplify in order to discover peace. So often we strive and work harder to connect with God but letting go can bring us connection and peace as well.

As we close week two of this Advent season, you are invited to take on a posture of presence with an embodiment exercise called a body scan. This activity helps increase awareness of breath and invites you to notice and release any tension you are holding in your body.

Lie on your back in a resting posture. You can lie down on your bed, the floor, or a yoga mat. Place one hand on your belly and one on your heart. Notice the rhythm of your breath. Notice your heartbeat. Notice how it feels to lie still for a few moments.

Allow your breath to deepen in your belly as you imagine a balloon inflating and deflating. Slowly expand your abdomen with each inhale and begin to lengthen your exhales. Observe any sensations, tension, or tightness in your body as you scan each part of the body. Breathe in as you notice each sensation and invite your body to relax. When you notice tension, tightness, pain, or stress, mentally send your breath to that part of your body and invite it to relax and rest in peace.

As you make your way to the top of your head, notice how your entire body feels. Move your awareness through each part of your body as you remain present. Release and relax your muscles by naming them to yourself or out loud. Follow the process below:

> Relax your feet.
> Relax your legs.
> Relax your buttocks.
> Relax your hips.
> Relax your abdomen.
> Relax your back.
> Relax your arms.
> Relax your hands.
> Relax your chest.
> Relax your shoulders.
> Relax your neck.
> Relax your head.

You may wish to practice this before bed or any time you begin to feel disconnected or overwhelmed. This exercise can help you release tension in the present and assist you in becoming more aware of tension or stress in your body when it arises in the future. For example, you could practice an abbreviated, seated version of this body scan at your desk or while traveling. Simply notice what cues your body is giving and make room for more peace within yourself.

Ponder and Go Forth

- Where were you holding tension in your body?
- As you released the tension and tightness, did you feel more peace in your body and spirit?
- What does peace feel like in your body?
- Are you able to trust your body enough to feel peace? Why or why not?

Closing Prayer for Week 2

God of wonder and peace, help me simplify in search of peace. Keep me present with you as I let go of expectations. Be present with me as I prepare myself and make room for your peace. Amen.

Sit with Joy

You have given me greater joy
than those who have abundant
harvests of grain and new wine.
—Psalm 4:7 (NLT)

We all know how it feels to be in a dark season of life. We all know what it feels like to struggle, to be anxious, to worry about the future. Perhaps you are going through a dark season right now. Whether that's the case or not, there is undoubtedly some uncertainty in your life. Joy may not feel familiar right now, and you may be left wondering, "How can I cultivate joy when I'm feeling like this?"

On the other hand, maybe you're living through a personally fruitful season with plenty of metaphorical grain and new wine, as in Psalm 4:7. Yet, alongside that fruitfulness, you may feel a bit of guilt or confusion as you recognize your privilege while living in a world that fosters poverty and division.

Maybe you're feeling a mix of emotions as you oscillate between highs and lows this season, between happiness and sadness. You're not sure what you feel from one moment to the next. It's conflicting to live in this tension between joy and struggle.

But isn't that exactly what Mary was feeling during the time before Jesus' birth?

Keep this in mind this week as you are invited to sit with joy. It's also vital for us to realize that joy is not happiness. Happiness happens to us. It is a feeling or an experience. Sometimes happiness isn't even all that great. A plateful of calorie-loaded fudge may bring me short-term happiness, but that doesn't mean that overindulging in a confectioner's delight is good for me or that my happiness is sustainable.

Joy, on the other hand, is a decision. Joy is an internally deep, purposeful choice to receive the gift God longs to cultivate in us. Scripture tells us that Christ's joy is already in us, "I have said these things to you so that my joy will be in you and your joy will be complete" (John 15:11, CEB). Our joy is not tied to our circumstances. Christ's joy is already in us, and that makes our joy complete, even in challenging times.

Advent joy is not without conflict. The story of Christ's birth includes threats against the life of our newborn Savior, yet we find deep joy in the promise of this story. Listen to Mary express her joy as you read her praise to God in Luke 1:46-55. Then, notice how she speaks into the future Jesus promises us today with these words from before Jesus was even born:

> "With all my heart I glorify the Lord!
>> In the depths of who I am I rejoice in God my savior.
> He has looked with favor on the low status of his servant.
>> Look! From now on, everyone will consider me highly favored

because the mighty one has done great things
for me.
Holy is his name.
He shows mercy to everyone,
from one generation to the next,
who honors him as God.
He has shown strength with his arm.
He has scattered those with arrogant thoughts
and proud inclinations.
He has pulled the powerful down from their
thrones
and lifted up the lowly.
He has filled the hungry with good things
and sent the rich away empty-handed.
He has come to the aid of his servant Israel,
remembering his mercy,
just as he promised to our ancestors,
to Abraham and to Abraham's descendants
forever." —Luke 1:46-55 (CEB)

This passage is a hymn of praise from Mary as she glorifies the Lord with joy. God has done great things for her. God has done great things for us. God will continue to do great things. Will you make room to go deep with joy this week?

Journal Prompt for Week 3

Consider a word, phrase, or image that Mary's words stir within you. Ponder the difference between joy and happiness in your life and write about that briefly. How will you choose to sit with joy this week?

Opening Prayer for Week 3

Creator God, show me how to sit with the highs and lows of joy and praise you deeply as Mary did. Amen.

DAILY PRACTICES FOR WEEK 3

Sit with Joy

Use any or all of this week's daily practices to sit with joy. Consider gathering items that bring you joy this week and either place them on a prayer altar or tape them in this book. Return to them as you work through these practices.

Day 1: Breath Prayer—Joy

As you breathe today, tip the corners of your mouth into a simple smile. Connect with the breath in your body by finding a comfortable posture (seated or reclined) and take full, deep breaths filling your diaphragm, then exhale completely. Place one hand on your heart and your other hand on your belly.

As you breathe in, expand your belly and say to
yourself: Lord
As you breathe out, deflate your belly and say to
yourself: I choose joy
Connect your inhale and exhale as well as your
words, offering your simple breath prayer to
God.

Repeat this prayer for five to ten minutes.

Inhale: Lord
Exhale: I choose joy

Ponder and Go Forth

- How does smiling, even for yourself, shift your prayer? Notice how this simple action offers you a few moments of joy.
- Journal or share what you notice in your body and your spirit with a friend or your small group.
- As you go about your day, breathe in and out purposefully, with a smile on your face, embodying God's gift of joy.

Day 2: Mindful Movement—Sing in Joy

Singing invites movement. When you sing, your breathing fluctuates as your vocal cords vibrate, creating a sound that resonates beyond your lips. Singing also activates your vagus nerve, a cranial nerve that connects the brain to the body. One of the longest nerves in the body, the vagus nerve travels from the skull to the abdomen and is responsible for sending signals in both directions throughout the body.[1] Activating the vagus nerve can send a signal to your body that it is time to de-stress. Therefore, no matter your ability to carry a tune, using your voice to sing or even hum connects your brain and body.

Giving yourself permission to sing is a mindful and accessible practice that can help you discover joy. You may even find yourself swaying your hips or moving your body. Singing also stimulates the pleasure center of your brain, so savor the process of singing and enjoy it! Take time to sing in the shower, in the car, or in your prayer space today as you ponder the following lyrics from Charles Wesley. Notice how the words invite us to focus on the arrival of our Messiah in the form of a baby and the joy of our longing hearts.

This hymn has been set to a variety of tunes over the years, so worry less about the melody and more about the movement of your voice. Whether or not you know the tune, sing this hymn or another song in joy today.

Come, thou long-expected Jesus,
Born to set thy people free;
From our fears and sins release us,
Let us find our rest in thee.
Israel's strength and consolation,
Hope of all the earth thou art;
Dear desire of every nation,
Joy of every longing heart.

Born thy people to deliver,
Born a child and yet a King,
Born to reign in us forever,
Now thy gracious kingdom bring.
By Thine own eternal spirit
Rule in all our hearts alone;
By thine all-sufficient merit,
Raise us to thy glorious throne.

"Come, Thou Long-Expected Jesus" by Charles Wesley (1744)

Ponder Go Forth

- Do you enjoy singing? Why or why not?
- Where do you like to sing? What inspires you to sing?
- What sensations do you feel in your body as you hum or sing? How does your body feel after singing?

Day 3: Lectio Divina—Hear Joy

Imagine seeing Jesus in human form! In Matthew 2:10-11, scripture tells us how the magi may have responded. Prepare yourself to respond today by inviting God to speak to you through the scripture.

Settle in and read Matthew 2:10-11 slowly, in *lectio divina* style. If listening to an audio recording of the scripture, consider sitting tall in a chair or finding a seated meditation pose.

Today's Scripture

When they saw the star, they were filled with joy. They entered the house and saw the child with Mary, his mother. Falling to their knees, they honored him. Then they opened their treasure chests and presented him with gifts of gold, frankincense, and myrrh.
—Matthew 2:10-11 (CEB)

Lectio (Read)—Slowly read or listen to Matthew 2:10-11 one time.

Meditatio (Reflect)—Read or listen to the passage again. Consider a word, phrase, or image from the passage that draws your attention. What stands out to you? Saw the star? Saw the child? Honored him? What do you hear, see, or sense? Reflect on how this word, phrase, or image speaks to you today. Consider repeating your word or phrase silently to yourself.

Oratio (Respond)—Read or listen to the passage one more time. Respond to what you hear in God's Word and how it makes you feel. Is there an invitation for you in the scripture today? Tell God what you heard or sensed.

Contemplatio (Rest)—Rest in what you have heard. Receive any clarity, stillness, insight, or imagery that comes to your mind. Give God thanks for this time, and rest in the Word of God.

Ponder and Go Forth

- What response do you have to joy?
- How does joy fill you?
- How might you be filled with joy as you anticipate the birth of the Christ child as Mary and the wise men did?

Day 4: Visio Divina—See Joy

Notice the joy emanating from the artwork, titled *Mary's Song,* on the following page. As you look at this image, note the first thing that draws your attention. Keep your gaze steady on

this part of the image for a minute or longer and breathe fully and deeply. What do you see?

Let your vision expand to the full image. Soak in the entire work of art and enjoy this time of contemplation. What else do you notice now? Her expression? Her hands? The background? Continue breathing fully and deeply as you reflect for another few minutes until you have absorbed the fullness of the art.

Take some time to respond to the following questions:

- What emotion does this artwork bring forth in you?
- How does this image prepare you to receive the gift of Christ this Advent season?
- What do you see in this artwork that speaks to your life today?
- How does this image help you see the invitation of joy?
- Does this experience invite you into a deeper form of prayer? If so, how?

You may wish to journal about your reflections, offer them to God in prayer, or simply remain silent for a few minutes.

Ponder and Go Forth

- How is joy expressed in this artwork?
- How is joy expressed in your own body? How might you carry a posture of joy into your day today?
- What does the color blue offer you as you ponder it?
- Notice the sun and the moon. Consider how they offer Mary light and joy. What do they offer you today?

Day 5: Christian Meditation—Sit in Joy

Most practitioners say it takes time and plenty of practice to find the joy in silent meditation. Now that you have practiced this a few times, notice if sitting in the quiet is more fulfilling than when you began just three weeks ago. Sit in an upright posture with your back supported and hands resting in your lap. If you choose, set a timer for however long you want to meditate.

Read Psalm 4:7 to center yourself and accept the invitation into God's presence.

> You have given me greater joy
> than those who have abundant harvests of grain and
>   new wine.
> —Psalm 4:7 (NLT)

Allow your eyes to close softly as you bring forth the word "joy" or another sacred word of your choosing.

Silently, with your eyes remaining closed, continue to repeat your sacred word. Breathe in and out with full, deep breaths. Let your mind settle as you allow your word to fade away and your body to become still in God's presence.

When thoughts surface or distractions arise, release them and return to your word. Let the repetition of that word draw your focus back to your quiet time with God.

Remain still and breathe for the duration of your time with God.

Offer an "Amen" to close your silent prayer.

Ponder and Go Forth

- How is your meditation practice changing you this Advent? Is it helping you cultivate more joy in your life?
- In what ways does silence make more room for joy?

Day 6: Creative Contemplation—Write Joy

You are already a poet by now! Again this week, you will use the space below to create an acrostic poem using the three letter word "joy." Remember, there is no right or wrong way to create this poem.

Take a few deep breaths to boost your creativity, then ponder the ways you have explored joy this week. Consider how you have been able to sit with joy during this Advent season.

Fill in your poem below:

J

O

Y

Use the following example if you need more inspiration.

Jesus was and is
Our gift from
You

Ponder and Go Forth

- Did you capture joy in just a few lines?
- Is embracing creativity joyful to you? Why or why not?

Day 7: Practicing Presence—Sense Joy

For most of us, food is a central part of any celebration. While our bodies need food for nourishment, they can also find great pleasure in the communal aspect of food. Mindful eating allows us to connect with our bodies as we move beyond eating for nourishment or habit or community and choose to savor the food we eat. Make space today to find joy in the food you eat, whether you are eating communally or alone. Follow these tips to use your sense of taste and be mindful and present in every bite:

- As you place food in your mouth, before chewing, notice how it tastes and feels.
- Consider the flavor and temperature of the food in your mouth as you savor the taste.
- As you chew slowly and mindfully, remain present with each bite.
- Give thanks to the one who prepared the food, where it came from, and how it arrived on your plate.
- Find joy not only in the taste of the food but in the process of being present during your meal.

Ponder and Go Forth

- Do you view food primarily as nourishment, a necessity, a habit, or a social activity? How does that affect your relationship to food?
- How might you sense more joy in your meals today?

Closing Prayer for Week 3

Giver of joy, in the depths of hard moments, bring me closer to you so that I may discover your joy. Allow me to make space for joy as I wait with you each day this season. Amen.

Savor God's Love

Tell me all about your faithful love come morning time,
because I trust you.
Show me the way I should go,
because I offer my life up to you.
—Psalm 143:8 (CEB)

The time is near. Christmas is almost here! God's gift of faithful love will be delivered to you this week in the form of a baby. While you may be tempted to rush through this final week before Christmas, I invite you to savor the gift of love, even as you go about your last-minute preparations.

Our bodies never tire of self-care and good habits. They crave the love we offer them each day. Consider sleep. Sleep is not something we can gather up on a Tuesday and then use to sustain ourselves for the remaining days of the week. In that same spirit, we are invited to cling to God's faithful love each and every day, allowing it to show us the path forward.

The longest night of the year falls during Advent. This presents us with a time to recognize the grief, loss, and hard times of the season, even as we are held in the love of God. In the long cold days of winter, how does God's love hold and sustain you? Have you noticed more love coming forth because of what we have already fostered this season—hope, peace, and joy?

The word "love" is a deep one with various meanings and usages in the English language. We use it for everything from romance to friends to an affinity for delicious food. We simply name it love.

To ponder what love looks like for us as Christians in Advent, let's continue to look to Mary. She experienced God's love in the midst of an overwhelming time filled with confusion and surprise, but also filled with the blessing that comes from being the birth mother of Christ (Luke 1:29-53). Mary's love for God is boundless! My pastor once said that Mary's love for Jesus made her Christ's first disciple. After all, Mary gave birth to God's love.

Jesus is God's love for the world and for us. If we ponder this invitation more deeply, we realize that the gift of love has a face and a name. We call it Jesus.

Chances are, you have held a baby you loved at some point in your life. That child could not comprehend your love, but your love was present nonetheless. Let us receive this kind of love from God this week, love beyond our own comprehension.

As you prepare to receive God's love this week, reflect on the words of Paul:

> I pray that you may have the power to comprehend, with all the saints, what is the breadth and length and height and depth and to know the love of Christ that surpasses knowledge, so that you may be filled with all the fullness of God. —Ephesians 3:18-19 (NRSV)

Journal Prompt for Week 4

As you reflect on God's love for you, journal about how it makes you feel and how you will savor it this Christmas. Consider sharing this with a spiritual friend or small-group companion.

Opening Prayer for Week 4

Holy One, allow me to fully savor the love you offer me this Christmas. Amen.

DAILY PRACTICES FOR WEEK 4

Savor God's Love

Use any or all of this week's daily practices to savor God's love. Consider gathering items that remind you of God's love this week and either place them on a prayer altar or tape them in this book. Return to them as you work through these practices.

Day 1: Breath Prayer—Love

Imagine God filling you with love as you breathe in, then imagine sharing that love with the world as you breathe out. Connect with the breath in your body by finding a comfortable posture (seated or reclined) and take full, deep breaths filling your diaphragm, then exhale completely. Place one hand on your heart and your other hand on your belly.

As you breathe in, expand your belly and say to
yourself: God
As you breathe out, deflate your belly and say to
yourself: I savor your love
Connect your inhale and exhale as well as your
words, offering your simple breath prayer to God.

Repeat this prayer for five to ten minutes.

Inhale: God
Exhale: I savor your love

Ponder and Go Forth

- Your brain is offered healing space when you make room for breathwork and prayer. Notice how this simple prayer connects you to the feeling of love, both for yourself and for others.
- Journal or share what you notice in your body and your spirit with a friend or your small group.
- As you go about your day, breathe in and out purposefully, savoring God's love.

Day 2: Mindful Movement—Dance in Love

People throughout history have found joy in dancing, even uncoordinated ones like me. We use dance to celebrate, commemorate, worship, and simply have fun! Dancing is also a fantastic stress reliever—whether we dance alone or with others. Dancing is good for your whole self.

Moving with mindfulness is an opportunity to notice how we move without judging our body. It also helps us practice love for our body as it moves. For this exercise, plan to dance alone so that you are not distracted by others moving alongside you. Whether you consider yourself a dancer or not, be willing to explore a bit and have some fun. Play as you dance and seek to embody God's love for you and your love for the one who created you.

Select a song that makes you want to dance, a song with a theme of love may add to your experience. As you begin to move with the music, notice what your body feels like as you connect with the rhythm of the song. Notice your heart rate and breathing intensify as you continue to move. Dance as long as you want, moving purposefully in love without judgment.

Ponder and Go Forth

- What is your relationship to dancing? Is dancing something that comes naturally to you, or do you struggle to dance and move freely?
- Do you have emotional, spiritual, or physical wounds that get in the way of enjoying dance? How can viewing dancing as a spiritual practice help you see it in a new light?
- How might God meet you in dance and help you lean into the love offered to you today?

Day 3: Lectio Divina—Hear Love

How do you hear love? Listen to God's Word today and see if you can notice what love sounds like. Prepare yourself to listen by inviting God to speak to you through the Scripture.

Settle in and read Luke 10:27 slowly, in *lectio divina* style. If listening to an audio recording of the scripture, consider sitting tall in a chair or finding a seated meditation pose.

Today's Scripture

He responded, *"You must love the Lord your God with all your heart, with all your being, with all your strength, and with all your mind, and love your neighbor as yourself."*
—Luke 10:27 (CEB)

Lectio (Read)—Slowly read or listen to Luke 10:27 one time.

Meditatio (Reflect)—Read or listen to the passage again. Consider a word, phrase, or image from the passage that draws your attention. Love the Lord? With all? Love your neighbor? Think about what stands out to you. What do you hear, see, or sense? Reflect on how this word, phrase, or image speaks to you today. Consider repeating your word or phrase silently to yourself.

Oratio (Respond)—Read or listen to the passage one more time. Respond to what you hear in God's Word and how it makes you feel. Is there an invitation for you in the scripture today? Tell God what you heard or sensed about love.

Contemplatio (Rest)—Rest in what you have heard. Receive any clarity, stillness, insight, or imagery that comes to your mind. Give God thanks for this time, and rest in the Word of God.

Ponder and Go Forth

- How do you love God with your whole self? What does that look like to you?
- Who is a neighbor you can offer God's love to this week? How might you show that person God's love?

Day 4: Visio Divina—See Love

Look upon the artwork, titled *Mary & Elizabeth*, on the opposite page. As you look at this image, note the first thing that draws your attention. Keep your gaze steady on this part of the image for a minute or longer while breathing fully and deeply. What do you see?

Let your vision expand to the full image. Soak in the entire work of art and enjoy this time of contemplation. What else do you notice now? Two women? Two lights in the womb? A dove? Continue breathing fully and deeply as you reflect for another few minutes until you have absorbed the fullness of the art.

Take some time to respond to the following questions:

- What emotion does this artwork bring forth in you?
- How does this image prepare you to receive the gift of Christ this Advent season?
- What do you see in this artwork that speaks to your life today?
- How does this image help you see the invitation of love?
- Does this experience invite you into a deeper form of prayer? If so, how?

You may wish to journal about your reflections, offer them to God in prayer, or simply remain silent for a few minutes.

Ponder and Go Forth

- Where do you see love in this image? Is this how you imagine Mary and Elizabeth looked at each other?
- From what you know of Mary and Elizabeth's stories, consider the way love is growing here.
- How do you embody love for your Creator? How does it feel to wait in this season for God's love?
- Do you see the light in their wombs? What does that light offer you today?

Day 5: Christian Meditation—Sit in Love

God's love for you is abundant! As you meditate today, cultivate your love for God in the silence. If you have become more comfortable with silence during this season, consider extending your time in the quiet today. Sit in an upright posture with your back supported and hands resting in your lap. If you choose, set a timer for however long you want to meditate.

Read Psalm 143:8 to center yourself and accept the invitation into God's presence.

Tell me all about your faithful love come morning
   time,
   because I trust you.
Show me the way I should go,
   because I offer my life up to you.
—Psalm 143:8 (CEB)

Allow your eyes to close softly as you bring forth the word "love" or another sacred word of your choosing.

Silently, with your eyes remaining closed, continue to repeat your sacred word. Breathe in and out with full, deep breaths. Let your mind settle as you allow your word to fade away and your body to become still in God's presence.

When thoughts surface or distractions arise, release them and return to your word. Let the repetition of that word draw your focus back to your quiet time with God.

Remain still and breathe for the duration of your time with God.

Offer an "Amen" to close your silent prayer.

Ponder and Go Forth

- Does sitting in the quiet allow you to feel God's love? Why or why not?
- Do you trust the love God offers you in the quiet? How does it affect you?
- How can you grow in that quiet trust of God's love?
- Consider the ways that love can guide your day today.

Day 6: Creative Contemplation—Write Love

Love poems are abundant but the one you write today need not be shared with anyone other than your Creator, unless you so desire. Use the space provided on the next page to create an acrostic poem using the word "love."

Take a few deep breaths to boost your creativity, then ponder the ways you have discovered love this week. Consider how you long to savor God's love during this Advent season.

Fill in your poem below

L

O

V

E

Use the following example if you need more inspiration.

Life is filled with
Opportunity to
Value
Everyone as being loved by God

Ponder and Go Forth

- How does it feel to write a love poem to God?
- Will you share it with God alone or will you share it with others? Why?

Day 7: Practicing Presence—Sense Love

Your hands are extensions of your being. They help you to give and receive God's love each and every day. Consider the number of times your hands have been folded in prayer, outstretched to help someone else, or simply been held by a loved one. In this posture of presence, you are invited to explore a hand meditation.

Bring to mind a person (or even a pet) that loves you. Imagine this love being extended to you now as you open your hands to receive it. Consider this love and then give thanks for the love that God has extended to you through the Christ child and the Incarnation of Christ. With open hands, prepare to receive this love as you offer your own love and life to God. With presence, recognize the gift of love, the gift of your body, and the gift of Christ.

With your hands resting open and palms up before you, gaze at your palms. What do you notice? Turn your hands palm down and see every detail. Do your hands remind you of the hands of a loved one? Are your hands a symbol of the work you do in this world or the work you are called to do?

Cup your open hands and tell God you are ready to receive the gift of Christ.

Ponder and Go Forth

- Has your appreciation for the miracle of your body deepened over the past four weeks?
- What has God shown you about loving and caring for yourself?
- How does God long to use your hands to share love with others?

Closing Prayer for Week 4

God, thank you for the gift of Jesus! Thank you for cultivating hope, peace, joy, and love within me this season! Allow me to carry these gifts forward as I savor and celebrate Jesus, your gift to humanity. Amen.

CONTEMPLATION BEYOND CHRISTMAS

"The problem is solved. Now go and utterly
enjoy all remaining days. Not only is it 'Always
Advent,' but every day can now be Christmas
because the one we thought we were just
waiting for has come once and for all."
—Richard Rohr[1]

You are ready! Our gift is here! And the best part? The gift of Christ's incarnation is one we continue to receive! Advent is only the beginning of Christmas. The season of Christmas, often called Christmastide, lasts for twelve days. However, this gift of God's presence can continue every day, even beyond Advent and Christmas. After all, the gift of Christ prepares us for all days to come. Our embodied journey with God never promised to be without trials, temptations, doubts, or struggles, so we invite Christ into each of our days as we choose to embody the hope, peace, joy, and love offered to us.

Spiritual embodiment allows us to fully live out our faith rather than merely checking off the box of religion. You have already accepted the invitation during the Advent season; why not accept the invitation to a contemplative life for the rest of the year? Contemplation is the act of deep reflective thought. One can be contemplative when enjoying food or spiritual reflection. You can watch sports in a meditative way or gaze upon backyard birds with a contemplative eye. I hear some people say that they would never describe themselves as contemplative people. Yet, I wonder if they simply have not yet found what they desire to contemplate. Consider these tips for continuing contemplative and embodied practices beyond the Advent season:

- Think about which of the contemplative practices in this book resonated with you the most. Consider how you can continue to use them going forward.
- Consider following the Christian calendar to become more aware of and more present in each season.
- Use your senses in worship, study, and when talking about your faith life with others. Our Christian tradition is much richer than words on a page. Think about how you embody your faith and live it out.
- Incorporate life-giving and embodied prayer practices into your daily life and invite others on the journey.
- Continue to practice mindfulness exercises that help you remain present and grounded with the person God created you to be!

As you consider the days to come, will you choose to engage on the contemplative journey with your whole self? Contemplation and embodiment benefit not only your relationship with God but the relationships you have with those around you. Contemplation in all seasons will draw you closer to your Creator and invite you to live into the person God created you to be. What a gift for the world!

SMALL-GROUP SUGGESTIONS

The four weeks of practices in this book are designed for individual reflection but may also be used in a small-group setting. Using one of the daily exercises each week, a small group could journey through the four weeks of Advent together. Each of the four individual themes can also be used in a small-group Advent workshop or a weekend retreat.

A small group may have one leader, or members of the group may take turns leading. If you are choosing a leader for your small group, consider asking someone with small-group leadership experience. This person should honor participants' time and respect different contemplative journeys.

It's also important to recognize that this book offers more questions than answers. Your time engaging with God in an embodied way will hopefully inspire a greater awareness of your whole self and a longing for more depth. But this devotional is not something you can complete; it is an exercise in drawing nearer to God through contemplation, a process that is always ongoing and in which we are always learning about God and ourselves.

Tips for Small-Group Leaders

- Create a sacred space for your small group. For example, light a candle and incorporate religious symbols or art into your time of reflection.
- Reduce distractions and consider using a sound machine or playing soft music if you are meeting in a space where distractions are prevalent.
- Honor participants' journeys and recognize the differences in their relationships with God and their relationships with their bodies.
- Open and close each group discussion in silence, focusing on the gift of breath.
- Allow space for participants to share their experiences and the ways God interacts with them on their spiritual journeys.
- Refrain from offering your own opinion, cross-talking, problem-solving, or fixing things. Instead, simply listen to the participants and be present.
- If you come together weekly, consider selecting and practicing just one of the daily exercises to participate in together as a group. Invite participants to share what they experienced while practicing the other exercises individually.
- Set aside time to journal together at the end of the session. Ask participants to reflect on what they have experienced individually and as a group each week.

Prayers

A Prayer for the Facilitator

Creator God, bless those who long to bring others closer to you this Advent. Allow them to see you at work in the lives of their companions. Give them the courage to lead, the vulnerability to share, and the capacity to care. Amen.

A Prayer for Participants

Loving God, we welcome into our lives those who come to listen more closely for you. May we honor the gift of the whole self—as you have created us. Thank you for the gift of Christ and your care for us. Allow us to be present with you and you among us this season of Advent. Amen.

CREATING SAFE SACRED SPACE FOR SMALL GROUPS

When gathering a small contemplative group, simple is always best! If you have significant interest in a group gathering, consider starting multiple groups or breaking out into smaller groups for discussion.

Simple refreshments are always fun but be careful not to take on too much. Being too hospitable to the appetite can sometimes cause us to lose opportunities to be hospitable to the soul. Food can be a great way to start and end your series as you break bread together to celebrate the bookends of your time. However, if it gets too complicated, it can become a distraction. Keep it simple or skip it altogether.

Each week drop an encouraging text message, handwritten note, or email to members of your group. Allow participants the space and time they need to embody the material (there is no race or timeline of expectations over these four weeks). The embodied journey can sometimes make us aware of our inner struggles, and it looks different for each of us.

Consider a simple and embodied outing together at the end of your four weeks—a bundled up walk in the park, practicing yoga together, or something similar.

What Is a Contemplative Group?

This type of small-group experience may be new for some participants since it is an invitation to a contemplative life.

Therefore, your time together will be less about answers and more about listening for God's voice with your whole self through contemplation.

Merriam-Webster defines contemplation as "concentration on spiritual things as a form of private devotion."[1] Consider how you can use the gift of embodiment to connect with God in a life of prayer and contemplation this Advent.

What Is Safe?

Due to the private nature of contemplation, a safe atmosphere is especially important for sharing. Consider the following guidelines and ask what else may be needed to offer a safe space for group listening and contemplation:

- Listen openly and without judgment.
- Share only what feels safe for you—and only about yourself. Do not share for or about others.
- Agree that what is shared will remain confidential.
- Be honest with yourself and with others.
- Reflect on what you hear, but do not offer advice.
- Ask your group what other sharing guidelines they wish to include and why.

Final Tips for Your Group

- Slow down.
- Let go of perfection.
- At the end of your gathering, sit in silence. Invite group members to pray silently for one another, and close with everyone saying "Amen."

You may wish to gather in a circle or simply offer signs of the peace of Christ to one another by name. Something like, "May the peace of Christ go with you, Elizabeth." To which is replied, "And also with you, David."

More than anything, I pray you savor and enjoy the process of offering safe spaces for others to meet God during this Advent season. May peace be with you!

Interactive Content

For interactive content related to this book visit the author's website at http://www.WhitneyRSimpson.com/Advent.

ACKNOWLEDGMENTS

To those who have supported me and the embodied ministry work I am called to share with others, my gratitude is never-ending. This Advent devotional is possible only because others have helped and encouraged me along the way. My thank you is authentic, and my gratitude runs deep for these soul friends:

Our Peace Seekers community from across the world who explored this Advent content with me as an online retreat prior to publication in book format.

My family, Troy and Drew, for their support and encouragement that allowed me time and space to escape and contemplate Christmas during the hot days of summer.

Bonnie Rushlow, my mom, and her artful eye through this book, most especially for the gift of all my special nativity ornaments.

My Upper Room Books peers, Sharon Seyfarth Garner, J. Dana Trent, and Kristen E. Vincent, for their nudge to submit this embodied content for publication.

Rev. Mary Anne Akin, my supervising mentor, for sharing her story and inspiring me with artwork, as well as always offering safe space along the way.

Leighanne Buchanan, my yoga business partner and friend, for helping me discover the importance of play amidst hard work and for encouraging both when under a deadline.

Rev. Stephen Handy, my pastor, for wise words that invited me to look more closely at Mary in order to meet Jesus today.

ACKNOWLEDGMENTS

The Upper Room Books team and a fantastic editor, Benjamin Howard, who helped me re-imagine this manuscript to better serve you, the reader. Thank you especially to Joanna Bradley Kennedy, who saw the vision for an embodied devotional book and helped it come to fruition, far better than I could have imagined. I have loved working with you on two books!

My Deaconess and Home Missioner community, my church family, peers, yoga teachers, professors, friends, and mentors who have impacted my own spiritual formation journey and who listen to my Enneagram Four feelings on a regular basis, you are appreciated more than you know, in all seasons.

Without Lauren Wright Pittman, I am not sure this devotional book would exist. Her artwork inspired my senses to create this embodied Advent experience.

NOTES

Introduction

1. Howard Thurman, *The Mood of Christmas* (Richmond, Indiana: Friends United Press, 1985) 21.
2. *Merriam-Webster*, s.v., "Advent," accessed September 12, 2021, https://www.merriam-webster.com/dictionary/advent.

Preparing for Christmas

1. *A Charlie Brown Christmas*, directed by Bill Melendez, (Media Home Entertainment, 1965).
2. Story permission from Rev. Mary Anne Akin.

Embodiment as Presence

1. Thomas Merton, *Thomas Merton, Spiritual Master*, ed. Lawrence S. Cunningham (New York: Paulist Press, 1992), 375.
2. Livia Shapiro, *The Somatic Therapy Workbook* (Berkeley, California: Ulysses Press, 2020), 16.
3. Amy G. Oden, *Right Here Right Now* (Nashville: Abingdon Press, 2017), 50.
4. Marcus J. Borg and John Dominic Crossan, *The First Christmas* (New York: HarperOne, 2007), 172.

Contemplative Practices to Explore

1. Claudia Mair Burney, *God Alone Is Enough* (Brewster, Massachusetts, Paraclete Press, 2010), 155.

2. Saint Teresa of Avila, *The Collected Works of St. Teresa of Avila, Volume 3*, ed. Otilio Rodriguez, trans. Kieran Kavnaugh (Washington, D.C.: Institute of Carmelite Studies, 1976), 96.

3. Donna Farhi, *The Breathing Book* (New York: Henry Holy and Company, 1996).

4. Whitney R. Simpson, *Holy Listening with Breath, Body, and the Spirit* (Nashville: Upper Room Books, 2016), 27.

5. Deirdre Fay, *Becoming Safely Embodied* (New York: Morgan James Publishing, 2021), 29.

6. David Emerson, *Trauma-Sensitive Yoga in Therapy: Bringing the Body into Treatment* (New York: W. W. Norton & Company, 2015), 7.

7. Simpson, *Holy Listening with Breath, Body, and the Spirit*, 23-24..

8. "Visio Divina," The Upper Room, accessed September 12, 2021, https://www.upperroom.org/resources/visio-divina.

9. Dwight H. Judy, *Christian Meditation and Inner Healing* (New York: The Crossroad Publishing Company, 1991), 9.

10. Thomas Keating, *Open Mind, Open Heart* (New York: Continuum Publishing, 2002).

11. Mary Elizabeth Williams, "Why Every Mind Needs Mindfulness," *Time Special Edition: Mindfulness*, December 2017, 10.

12. J. Dana Trent, *One Breath at a Time* (Nashville, Upper Room Books, 2019).

13. Brother Lawrence, *The Practice of the Presence of God* (Mansfield Centre, Connecticut: Martino Publishing, 2016), 27.

How to Use This Devotional

1. Nadia Bolz-Weber, *Pastrix* (Nashville: Jericho Books, 2013), 86.

Slow Down and Hope

1. Sara Smith, "5-4-3-2-1 Coping Technique for Anxiety," Behavioral Health Partners Blog, University of Rochester Medical Center, accessed September 12, 2021, https://www.urmc.rochester.edu/behavioral-health-partners/bhp-blog/april-2018/5-4-3-2-1-coping-technique-for-anxiety.aspx.

Sit with Joy

1. Trent, *One Breath at a Time*, 31.

Contemplation Beyond Christmas

1. Richard Rohr, *Preparing for Christmas* (Cincinnati: Franciscan Media, 2013), 93.

Creating Safe Sacred Space for Small Groups

1. *Merriam-Webster*, s.v., "Contemplation," accessed September 12, 2021, https://www.merriam-webster.com/dictionary/contemplation.

ABOUT THE AUTHOR

Deaconess Whitney R. Simpson is the founder of Exploring Peace Ministries. She is a soul care practitioner, helping others reach their fullest human potential as they explore the gift of God's peace. Whitney is a trained spiritual director, yoga and meditation teacher, and the author of *Holy Listening with Breath, Body, and the Spirit*. Whitney holds space for others to meet God through embodied spirituality and the ministry of spiritual formation. Discover more of her ministry offerings at ExploringPeace.com. You can connect with Whitney directly at WhitneyRSimpson.com.

About the Artist

Rev. Lauren Wright Pittman is the Director of Branding and Founding Creative Partner of Sanctified Art, a ministry providing multimedia creative resources for church leaders and spiritual seekers. Lauren is a visual artist, graphic designer, and visual exegete. She uses paint, metallic inks, linoleum carving tools, and Apple pencil to image the layered complexity she experiences in scripture. Lauren's work can be found at sanctifiedart.org and lewpstudio.com

Printed in the USA
CPSIA information can be obtained
at www.ICGtesting.com
LVHW070747161023
760909LV00019B/14